FOCUS ON THE FAMILY®

renewing the heart™

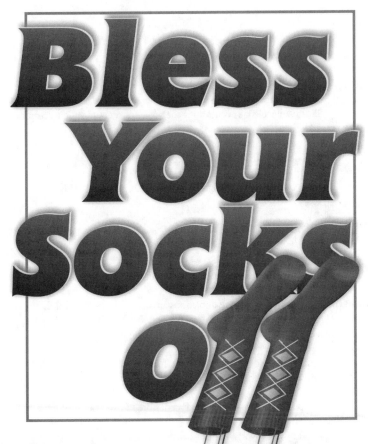

Bless Your Socks Off

Unleashing the Power of Encouragement

Sandra Picklesimer Aldrich

D1053943

Tyndale House Publishers, Wheaton, Illinois

BLESS YOUR SOCKS OFF

Library of Congress Cataloging-in-Publication
Aldrich, Sandra Picklesimer.
        Bless your socks off : unleashing the power of encouragement / Sandra
Picklesimer Aldrich.
        p.   cm.
        Includes bibliographical references.
        ISBN 1-56179-579-8
        1. Encouragement—Religious aspects—Christianity. I. Title.
BV4647.E53A43   1998
241'.4—dc21   97-47627
                                                                        CIP

Published by Tyndale House Publishers, Wheaton, Illinois.

The author is represented by the literary agency of Alive Communications,
1465 Kelly Johnson Blvd., Suite 320, Colorado Springs, CO 80920.

Editor: Michele A. Kendall
Cover Design: Bradley L. Lind

Printed in the United States of America

98 99 00 01 02 03 04/10 9 8 7 6 5 4 3 2 1

*To all those who have
lovingly encouraged me over the years—
especially Bobbie Valentine, my dear friend,
who repeatedly "sat shiva" with me*

Sandra Picklesimer Aldrich is one of Dianna's and my favorite people. We have found her encouraging even when she has been in the darkest valleys of life's journey. Read *Bless Your Socks Off* and be encouraged.

—Jerry B. Jenkins, author of
the *Left Behind* series

Sandra Aldrich has done it again! With humor, practicality, honesty, and "down-home" warmth, she has written a book that will touch your heart and give you the tools for impacting others with inspiration, hope, and encouragement. I laughed and cried as she wove poignant illustrations into the content of every chapter. The "Quick Encouragement" sections give the reader practical ways to implement personal change, and the added discussion questions make this book an excellent choice for small groups. *Bless Your Socks Off* is a must-read book for growing Christians. I highly recommend it.

—Carol Kent, speaker and author
of *Secret Longings of the Heart*

Sandra Aldrich is one of the most popular speakers booked by CLASS. Her down-to-earth humor and honest message touch the hearts of all who hear her. As you read *Bless Your Socks Off*, you will experience firsthand what makes Sandra so popular. Her [speaking] style translates wonderfully to the printed page, making *Bless Your Socks Off* a quick but powerful read.

—Marita Littauer, president
of CLASServices Inc., speaker, and
author of *Personality Puzzle*

Contents

Introduction:
A Letter to a Friend

*D*ear Friend,

Each autumn, I joyfully anticipate the southern migration of the Canada geese over our community. As I watch the great flocks gather in V-formations, I marvel at their majestic grace—and constant honking. I've read that the strongest bird takes the lead, creating an updraft for the ones behind it. Then as the leader tires and drops back, another bird takes its place, heading into the wind. Those who write about the great birds tell us that the weak ones actually are in the middle, surrounded by those who are stronger, and thus are protected from dropping behind. Together the flock flies farther than each bird could alone. Also, the honking is not random noise, but encouragement from one to another to keep going.

In the fall of 1992, I learned in a personal way just how important sounds of encouragement can be. I was speaking at a little church in my beloved home state of Kentucky. Anyone who's with me for more than a few minutes knows that talking is not difficult for me, but that evening, as I looked at the audience—several of whom were my third and fourth cousins—I was suddenly aware of life's numerous hiccups. If consecutive seasons' low crop prices hadn't forced my family to move from our farm in the early 1950s, I would have grown up knowing those cousins by more than just name. Suddenly, I felt both an incredible kinship and an incredible loss.

In one of those rare occasions when I'm choked up publicly, tears threatened to spill onto my cheeks, and I couldn't speak. I was embarrassed, of course, but the audience looked at me lovingly, as though they understood my tumbling thoughts. A few spoke aloud: "That's all right, honey," and "Help her, Lord." The audible comments momentarily startled me, but I took a deep breath, smiled my thanks, and continued my talk.

Since that evening, I've thought about the strength those kind faces and encouraging words gave me. And I've recalled other times in my life when someone cheered me on with a patient "Hey, you *can* do this." Encouragers come in various forms, and their pats on the back—tangible or verbal—can be planned or spontaneous, but they always carry the potential to change circumstances and sometimes even lives.

Have you had a dose of encouragement today? No? Then let the following pages convey my come-here-I'm-glad-to-see-ya bear hug! In my half century of living, I've learned a few things about encouragement, and I want to share them with you. As you're reading about these experiences, imagine that I've greeted you at my front door and invited you into the kitchen, where gingerbread fresh from the oven is waiting. I want you to feel special—because that's exactly what you are!

Sandra Picklesimer Aldrich
Colorado Springs, Colorado

The Power That Changes Lives

Patsy Clairmont, popular speaker and author of several insightful books, including *God Uses Cracked Pots* and *Normal Is Just a Setting on Your Dryer*, had finished recording the cassette version of her latest work as I stepped into the studio lobby. She invited me to sit with her, and we chatted briefly about our having lived within just a few miles of each other during my Michigan days. Gradually, our conversation turned to Jill Renich-Meyers, a mutual friend.

"Years ago, neighbors took me to Jill's Bible class," Patsy said. "I loved the Lord, but I was difficult to get along with back then, since my poor self-image wouldn't allow me to believe that others could really love me. My long-suffering friends, who tolerated my nit-picking, probably hoped I'd get a few tips on how to get along better with others. Instead, that class completely changed my life!

"Jill is the first person who ever told me I had any worth," Patsy continued. "She mentioned after one class that she found my comments interesting, adding, 'I believe that you will one day be a writer.' No one had ever said anything like that to me before. Suddenly, I was hopeful that I might be useful in God's kingdom after all. If it hadn't been for her, I never would have dared to go through any of the doors the Lord was opening."

Encouragement profoundly changed Patsy's life and, in turn, allowed her to encourage countless others through her Milk (nourishment) and Honey (encouragement) Ministry. But what if Jill hadn't bothered to point out Patsy's potential? What if she had merely commented to her family over dinner that she had an interesting student? (Alas, many of us have a tendency to be like the husband who loved his wife so much he *almost* told her!) But the good news is, Jill did verbalize Patsy's potential, and that encouragement reproduces itself every day through Patsy's ministry.

Encouragement's Power

How would a few words of affirmation change your day—or your life? I'm convinced that the need for encouragement—the longing to hear someone cheer us on—is part of our human makeup. Think about the child just learning to walk. He pulls himself up at the sofa, then grins and looks around to see if anyone is watching. As his audience responds with outstretched arms and calls of "Come on, come on," he takes a hesitant step. If his effort is rewarded with hand-clapping or a robust "All right!" he is more apt to try again.

That need to be encouraged doesn't stop after we learn to walk. Those who have accomplished much often credit the encouragement of others—whether a quiet "I know you can do this, honey," or enthusiastic cheers from the crowd—for all they've managed to do. No matter what the exterior shows, inwardly we all need that little "Yes, you can" push that makes the difference in our lives. In fact, even simple encouragement has incredible power to change lives—emotionally, spiritually, physically—heal relationships, and give hope.

Encouragement Can Lift Another's Spirits

Years ago, my family and I were vacationing at a Bible conference in Michigan. That was back when I was awed by anyone who had a public ministry, so each time I saw one of the speakers or guest musicians on the grounds, I'd merely smile. I didn't dare actually greet them.

Then one week, a musical family was on the program. Their talents ranged from deeply spiritual hymns played on the piano, organ, and violin, to peppy choruses produced as they ran their fingertips over crystal glasses filled with varying amounts of water. We never knew what to expect—some nights serious, some nights hilarious—but the concerts were always wonderful.

One morning, I saw the father of this talented group approaching. He was walking slowly, with downcast eyes and slumped shoulders.

I hesitated to intrude, but I took a quick breath and said, "We've so enjoyed your music this week. Thank you for being here."

He smiled. "I really appreciate that."

As he walked on, I noticed—to my great surprise—that his shoulders were straighter and his step livelier.

I was so astounded by the difference my few words had made that I began to look for other opportunities to offer sincere compliments. Sometimes I'd point out something special the Bible study teacher had said, or send our pastor a midweek note, or tell a friend how I appreciated her patience with her young children. Each time, the words had a strengthening effect upon the receiver.

Encouragement Makes the Future Brighter

Actually, I'm amazed that I was so slow in understanding encouragement's power. After all, a few kind words when I was only 12 had given me the vision to get an education. The summer before I entered seventh grade, I met Doris Schumacher, a teacher visiting her elderly aunt Minnie, who lived across the street from my family.

Schoolteachers frightened me because several of mine had ridiculed my Southern speech patterns, so I was immediately intimidated by Doris, too.

But she smiled and said, "Aunt Minnie tells me

you're going into junior high this fall. Tell me, what do you like to study?"

I was surprised by her question. I usually heard only "How's school?" from adults.

I managed, "Well, I like to read, and I like history."

She smiled again, and her graying hair seemed like a halo. "That's wonderful," she said. "I teach eighth-grade English and social studies in Minneapolis. What do you like to read?"

Two direct questions from an adult! Stammering, I told her about the books I had read that past week.

She nodded approvingly. "Good choices," she said. Then as I turned to leave, she added, "I assume that you're nervous about going into junior high. Don't be; you'll do just fine!"

The conversation probably had taken all of three minutes, but by the time I walked across the street and up our front steps, I was determined to be a teacher "just like Doris!"

In the 1950s, none of the women in my extended family had attended college, so my announcement was a bit unsettling to some of the relatives. But I pulled the dream into my heart and, with God's grace and my perseverance, gained the B.A. and M.A. degrees that gave me 15 years in a Detroit-area classroom. Later, those same degrees opened the door for me to pursue an editing career and rebuild my life after my husband died.

Doris is 94 now, but she has continued to encourage me over the decades. One snowy morning, years ago, as we chatted over long-distance lines, she commented about how far I had come since my school days.

"You're a big part of that success," I said. "You gave me the vision to go to college." Then I began to tell her about that long-ago three-minute meeting.

She interrupted me. "No, dear," she said. "The first time I met you was when you were 15 and visiting Aunt Minnie at the hospital after she'd broken her hip."

"Oh, no, Doris," I insisted. "I was 12. I remember you stood by the oak table in her front room. The morning sun was coming through the lace curtains and falling across your brown and gray sweater that so beautifully matched your hair just beginning to turn gray."

She sighed, then said, "Oh, my dear, I don't remember that at all."

I chuckled. "It's okay, Doris," I said. "That morning only changed my life!"

Truly her kindness had done exactly that.

Encouragement Can Heal Physically

My friend Donna Melby has seen encouragement's power to heal. She first met Charlie in the Sunday school class she helped lead for the handicapped. Because of his small size, Donna thought he was five. He was actually 16. He had been neglected as a baby and badly malnourished when he was discovered by the court and placed in the state hospital. He had grown up there, and his loving attitude despite his deformed legs had quickly won the heart of Donna's coworker, a nurse at the institution, who brought him to their class.

As Donna came to know Charlie better, her heart opened wide to him, and gradually her family began to include him in their activities. One day they decided to take him to the zoo. The ward nurse had outfitted him in a pair of cowboy boots for the event, so Donna planned to replace those with a pair of her son's tennis shoes. She gasped as she pulled off the boots and saw Charlie's skinny, twisted legs and feet. They wouldn't fit in normal shoes.

Well, she decided, at least she could get him a cooler shirt. She led him into three-year-old Brent's room and pulled a short-sleeved outfit out of the drawer. It fit perfectly. A toddler and a 16-year-old both in size five.

The Melbys continued to see Charlie at church each week that fall, and for Christmas they welcomed him for a two-week visit. The more time they spent with him, the more they loved him. Eventually, they decided he had to be a permanent part of their family. It took nine months to work out the details, but Charlie finally—and officially—became part of the Melby family.

Donna and her husband, Otto, enrolled Charlie in the district's excellent special-education program. He boarded the school bus every morning in front of their house. They also took him to a clinic specializing in leg deformities, where they came up with custom shoes.

Then Charlie began to grow. When he first came to live with the Melbys, his height and weight had been the same: 39 inches tall and 39 pounds. Fifteen months later, he had grown 18 inches. As he grew, his legs began to straighten so that it was easier for him to walk. He was changing before their very eyes! He was still short, and the early brain damage caused by the malnourishment was still evident, but his legs were strong.

Finally, after following the case closely for two-and-a-half years, the doctor at the clinic checked Charlie's straightened legs, shook his head in amazement, and said, "You don't have to bring him in anymore." Then he asked, "To what do you attribute this miraculous growth and bone straightening?"

Eagerly, Donna told how Charlie had come to live with them. They were convinced, she said, that God's touch and the love and encouragement of a family had unleashed the little boy's growth.

The doctor rolled his eyes, cleared his throat, and turned to dictate into his tape recorder: "The mother says the healing comes from some religious experience. Case closed."

But for the Melby family, that's one case that will never be closed because they know their love, care, and encouragement made a profound difference in one little boy's life.[1]

I can think of numerous other examples of how encouragement and love healed broken bodies—HIV babies who showed no evidence of the disease after being cared for by a loving adoptive family, Romanian orphans who responded wonderfully to hands-on care after years of neglect, premature babies whose vital signs improved when they were soothingly touched and talked to, stroke victims who made remarkable recoveries when they had a supportive family cheering them on. We have access to more of encouragement's power than we can imagine.

Encouragement Can Repair Relationships

In addition to healing bodies, encouragement can heal relationships. I remember a woman, Grace, who listened intently at a church retreat as the speaker said it was up to her to get the communication ball rolling with her spouse. The speaker suggested that the best way to do that was not by saying, "Why don't we ever talk?" but by giving her man a compliment.

Grace was doubtful. Her husband was always grumpy; also, he didn't like people, particularly her. He was rigid in his demands and unforgiving when they weren't met. For example, his arrival home from work each evening was to be met with supper served exactly at 5:30, or he would grouch the rest of the evening.

A few days after attending the seminar, Grace decided to make the first move toward reconciliation. She racked her brain for something positive she might say to her husband that would be sincere. Finally, that evening as she set his filled plate before him, she said, "Today I was thinking about how you worked all those odd jobs to keep a roof over our heads when the plant closed. I really appreciated that, but I've never told you. I guess I was too busy worrying about stretching every dollar."

She glanced at him, expecting to see his usual frown. To her amazement, his eyes were glistening with tears. Someone had recognized his efforts. In the weeks that followed, this couple began to make significant strides in communication because of the wife's willingness to find a way to break the barrier between them.

Sometimes all it takes to restore a damaged relationship is an offhand comment. One of my Detroit friends worked with two women who were constantly at odds. One afternoon, he casually said, "I don't understand these emotional potshots. Both of you are nice people." His encouraging perspective seemed to turn on a little light within each woman, and the snide remarks stopped.

Grace and my friend made a wise choice when they decided to concentrate on finding the good in people rather than focusing on their weaknesses. The book of Proverbs offers at least two verses to remind us of the destruction that can come from fueling emotional fires. In Proverbs 16:28, we read, "A perverse man stirs up dissension, and a gossip separates close friends." Proverbs 26:20 further says, "Without wood a fire goes out; without gossip a quarrel dies down." Haven't we all known situations in which a person kept the flames raging by constantly criticizing someone or contributing to gossip? It takes someone special to put out emotional fires.

Encouragement Can Ease the Challenges of Life

Encouragement can help us move more easily through major challenges in our lives—as my dad learned in North Platte, Nebraska, during World War II.

It was May 1945, and he was a 24-year-old army sergeant on a Maryland troop train heading west; the men's ultimate destination was the war in the South Pacific. The days on the train were tedious. It stopped in small towns only to take on provisions and let the soldiers stretch their legs. Often it had to pull onto a side track to wait for a lumbering freight train to precede it over a bridge. (The military wouldn't risk sending a loaded troop train over what might prove to be a dynamited structure.)

The soldiers had been on board for several days when one morning just before six o'clock, the train pulled into North Platte. As the men clambered onto the platform to work the kinks out of their cramped muscles, homemakers came running toward them, bearing coffee pots and whatever homemade baked goods they'd had in their cupboards. Several of the women still had curlers in their hair and bathrobes on.

For the next several minutes, friendly pandemonium reigned as wives, mothers, and kid sisters thrust cups of black coffee and wedges of pie and cake into eager, outstretched hands. The introductions were quick: "Where you from, soldier?" or "I'm Millie. If you meet my boy Jake, tell him we're praying for him."

All too soon, the train whistle blew, and the soldiers were ordered back on board. The women cheered and called out blessings to them as the train pulled out of the station. Upon reaching the Philippines, the men were able to carry that morning's encouragement with them into battle. For those like my dad who came home, the memory of that morning lingers years later, and each time the story is retold, it's a reminder that even the simplest gestures can transmit encouragement's power.

Encouragement Can Help Spread the Good News of Salvation

I remember a poster from the 1960s: An unkempt old man in a wrinkled suit is sitting on a park bench. His eyes are downcast, his chin covered with gray stubble. The caption reads, "You told me about the love of God, and then you went on your way."

Many of us find it easier to perform discrete acts of encouragement rather than living each day encouraging those around us. It's far more convenient to occasionally write a check for a special cause or make a meal for a neighbor than to commit to volunteering at the city homeless shelter every weekend. That's why I love the example of Barnabas—the first person from the Scriptures we think of when we hear the word "encouragement." His name originally was Joseph, but the apostles changed it to one that meant "son of encouragement" (Acts 4:36). He's described as "a good man, full of the Holy Spirit and faith" (Acts 11:24), who daily did practical, tangible things to encourage people.

Barnabas wasn't someone who encouraged only when it was convenient. He dared to accept Paul after the Damascus Road experience when everyone else ostracized him (Acts 9:27–28). Think about that: Here was Paul, formerly Saul of Tarsus, an unrelenting persecutor of the early church. He even had been

present at—and undoubtedly participated in—the ston-
ing of Stephen (Acts 7). So who can blame the believ-
ers for their caution? But Barnabas was willing to
welcome the newcomer.

And that encouragement extended to others, too.
In Acts 15:36–40, Barnabas insisted that Paul give
young John Mark another chance after the lad had
abandoned Paul in a previous journey (Acts 13:13).
This disagreement between Paul and Barnabas became
so intense that the two older men actually parted
company for a while.

I'm thankful the story didn't end there. Later in
2 Timothy 4:11, Paul writes, "Get Mark and bring him
with you, because he is helpful to me in my ministry."
The Scriptures don't tell us how John Mark and Paul
reestablished their relationship, but surely Barnabas, the
encourager, had a part in it.

Not only does this account show the combined
power of forgiveness and encouragement to show
Christ's love to others, but it also provides an example
of how our actions can prepare others to receive the
good news of salvation. And isn't that the greatest
encouragement of all?

The preceding stories—one woman pointing out the
strengths of another, a timid expression of appreciation, life-changing kindnesses, and even physical healing—all show encouragement's power to make a
decided difference in another's life. My goal as you
read this book is that you'll see the importance of

encouragement in this intense world and also begin to encourage yourself and offer that life-changing encouragement to others.

Quick Encouragement

1. Our physical and emotional strength can actually increase if someone encourages us when we're tired or disheartened.
2. No matter what the exterior shows, inwardly we all need that little "Yes, you can" push that makes the difference in our lives.
3. Encouragement can give hope for a brighter future.
4. Encouragement has the power to heal bodies as well as relationships.
5. Many of us find it easier to do an occasional loving thing than to *be* loving.
6. Barnabas helped spread the good news of salvation by showing others the importance of encouraging and believing in one another.

Discussion Questions

1. What power does encouragement have in your life?
2. Who has been of particular encouragement to you? David, Martha,
3. Have you seen encouragement and love heal someone physically?
4. Can you think of a particular encouragement that changed your life?

5. Has anyone ever taken a chance on you the way Barnabas did with Paul? If so, what were the results? *Christ*
6. What biblical personality offers special encouragement to you?
7. In what ways can/do you encourage others? →

Notes

1. Donna Melby, "Charlie's Best Stone," *Christian Herald* (March 1989): 22.

Encouraging
Yourself

During a tour of Dearborn, Michigan's Greenville Village, the guide took us into Henry Ford's childhood home and quoted the great industrialist as having said, "Whether you think you can or you can't, you'll be right."

Since that long-ago tour, I've had numerous opportunities to prove the truth of those words. In fact, three years after my husband died, I became one of the growing number of women who change careers in midlife, when I left the security of teaching in Michigan to become an editor in New York. Even though I was excited about the opportunity, it didn't take long for me to miss the familiarity of our Midwest community and my own classroom. Worst of all, I missed being a beloved wife.

One afternoon I was struggling with a story about

Charles Sheldon, the author of the classic *In His Steps*.
I couldn't get a precise caption for the accompanying
photograph. My boss finally intervened.

As I gave up my seat at the computer to him, I
kiddingly said, "If I were younger, I'd just get remarried
and have babies. I know how to do that."

He barely glanced at me as he said, "You can do
this." Then he proceeded to show me how to make the
needed caption fit the space limitation.

Instruction accomplished, he returned to his desk
while I pondered his comment. He was right: If I could
leave all that was familiar to move my family to New
York, I certainly could write captions. In that moment, I
turned his offhand comment into my personal encouragement. Soon, I was tackling projects with a quick
prayer and a muttered "I can do this."

That is the gift I want you to give yourself, too.
Remember, "Whether you think you can or you can't,
you'll be right."

Steps to Encouragement

Over the years, I've learned to open myself to encouragement in several ways. I hope you'll find the following
principles helpful as well.

1. Take Off Your Mask

One of the joys of living a long time is learning how
ridiculous it is not to be honest with yourself about the
person you are. I remember preparing to speak at a
women's retreat and praying, "Lord, help me show

these women how to remove their masks." Then, stung by the self-righteousness of that request, I immediately amended my prayer: "No, Lord, help me to remove my mask."

In that moment, God—with His wild sense of humor—surely said, "Okay!" and I forgot my makeup! The retreat was in the Rocky Mountains, so I couldn't just run across the street and buy what I needed. And I wasn't about to borrow someone else's makeup.

As I fretted about what to do, I realized this was the answer to my prayer. So, faceless, I stood before the group and explained my prayer as the reason for their not being able to see my eyes. Then I began to talk about some of the masks we hide behind at one time or another, including control, happiness, self-righteousness, and perfectionism.

Later, one of the women wrote to me about the effect this particular speech had on her:

> In an instant I was stripped to the bone, and I was sobbing on the inside as you said, "Let's take off the masks." My husband and I have leadership positions within the church, but everything I do has to be "perfect" or I'm miserable—and miserable to live with—for weeks. I couldn't let people know who I really am since I was afraid they wouldn't like me. But I don't think they like me very much now. Your getting up in front of all those women without your makeup really got my attention, especially as I realized I would have canceled the retreat before I would have done

that. Now I'm asking God to show me how to take off my mask, but I hope He's gentler with me than He was with you.

I chuckled at her last sentence and was sorry she hadn't signed her name. How I would love to know how the Lord answered her prayer! But I do know that her freedom—and mine—began with the realization that we don't have to be "perfect" before the Lord can use us.

2. Make a List of Your Good Qualities

And don't say you don't have any! It's that type of thinking that gets us into emotional messes. Instead of thinking we can't do anything right, let's pretend that we're impartial talent scouts who will list those things that are true about our characters. Try it. Describe your abilities, achievements, curiosity about the world, and considerate treatment of others.

Too often we have a tendency to disregard our own gifts and want the gifts others have. When I list my abilities, I still struggle over the fact that I can't play the piano. After all, "proper" Christian women are musical, right? But as I concentrate on the things I can do instead of those I can't, I get to list public speaking. I can stand in front of 5,000 people, and my heart won't skip a beat.

Judy struggled with listing what she could do, too. Finally, she wrote, "I can understand complicated dress patterns." Understand? I'll say! She can construct an outfit that rivals any designer creation. (When I wear the things in public that I've sewn, women always smile graciously and say, "Oh, did you make that?")

If Alice were to show us her list, she'd lament that it took her forever to put even one thing down because she was so busy thinking of the things she can't do. When she finally talked herself into thinking of the things she *can* do, she listed "Give a great whistle." Having freed herself from listing "proper" activities, she had fun writing down such things as changing her own oil, making Southern spoon bread that calms her husband when he's upset, cutting fancy paper dolls freehand for their daughters, and hanging wallpaper without getting impatient. That simple little list started her grinning, and from there she began feeling better about herself.

How encouraging we could be to ourselves if we would honestly appreciate our own skills! And it's only when we can truly appreciate our own talents that we'll be able to appreciate the talents of others.

3. Focus on Your Blessings

After my husband, Don, died of cancer at the age of 39, it would have been easy for me to withdraw from life, but I didn't want to be one of those hand-wringing widows who go through life telling everyone that their grief is greater than any other people have experienced. So, one lonely, fear-filled evening, I forced myself to list my blessings, beginning with my two young children, who depended on me. Then my list named friends and extended family and emphasized that I had few bills and a low mortgage payment on the house. I finished the list with the blessing that I could hope that the backyard again would be filled with daffodils in the spring.

Of course, the list doesn't have to result from grief or desperate loss. Sometimes all we're dealing with is a "blue day" that needs the tangible and simple act of reminding ourselves of our blessings—and that our situation is not as desperate as we think it is.

4. Try to Find the Positive in Difficult Situations

When confronted by an unpleasant situation, sometimes it helps to find something you can be thankful for in it. One of my young friends and her roommate were traveling in Europe via rental car. One afternoon after stopping at a rest area, they came back to the car after only a few minutes and discovered the trunk and all the doors open. Everything was gone: all their luggage, both cameras, and their souvenirs.

They reported the theft to the police, who merely shrugged and asked why the car had been left unattended. Dejected, the girls checked into a hotel to await the morning and ponder their next action. As they sat crying on their beds, my friend reached into her purse to get a tissue.

Suddenly, she smiled. "Wait a minute. At least my purse wasn't stolen. That means I've still got my plane ticket and my passport."

The other girl grabbed her own purse and dumped its contents onto the bed. "Look! I've still got the necklace I bought for Mom's birthday. And the pictures of all of my nieces and nephews when they were babies. And here's my favorite lipstick!"

Their tears dried as the two girls counted everything they still possessed. Oh, their stolen goods didn't suddenly appear, and they still had to decide what to do about the rest of their trip, but they slept soundly that night and were better able to think about their options the next morning.

Those two women faced an immediate crisis, but sometimes our challenges are ongoing. In one of my visits to the Red Bird Mission in Beverly, Kentucky, I learned that a well-known men's underwear company sent a train carload of "fourths" to the mission. We all buy "seconds" and sew up the seams, but this shipment was several quality grades below that—which meant that a shoulder seam might run across the front of the shirt, or a gaping hole might appear on the back. Awful though the donation was, the little mission got busy with finding ways to use the material: The craft women braided them into rugs, made them into polishing cloths for car kits, and so on. Finally, the supply was depleted, and everyone sighed with relief that they had been good stewards of the gift.

Then another train carload showed up! One of the secretaries called the director of the mission about the new shipment and said in a tired voice, "Another load of those old, ugly shirts came in."

Suddenly, a light went on in someone's head, and with a little green screening paint, those shirts were turned into one of the best-selling items in the craft store. What's screened on them? *Red Bird Ugly Shirt!* And all because someone looked at the situation in a new way.

5. Have Faith in Yourself

My maternal grandmother, Mama Farley, understood that if we think we can't do something, we're already defeated. In fact, she summarized the King James Version of Proverbs 23:7a—"For as he thinketh in his heart, so is he"—with her own interpretation: "Believin' makes it so." If I said I couldn't possibly get the dumplings right, she'd add a quiet "Believin' makes it so, honey," as she checked the amount of flour I planned to use. She refused to let any of her grandchildren accept defeat before we had exhausted every creative solution. (Of course, if no solution was possible, she had a saying for that, too: "There are some things in life that all you can do with 'em is bear 'em.")

Years later, when I'd captured my dream of becoming a classroom teacher, I read a study that proved the importance of helping children believe in themselves. Unfortunately, I've forgotten its name, but I do remember that it involved giving all the students a test and then reporting to the teachers *higher* scores for those students who had received the lowest ones. Since the teachers believed the students could do a better job—and told them they were intelligent enough to tackle any challenge—the students believed it also and unfailingly lived up to their teachers' expectations.

6. Set Goals and Work Toward Them

Mable, an elderly friend, modeled this principle for me when she enrolled in college when she was in her eighties. She had raised her family, helped her widowed daughter raise hers, and then decided it was time to do what she'd always wanted to do: get an education. She did exactly that, majoring in history. When she died in her nineties, she had been making plans to work on her master's degree.

If a goal you've set seems unachievable, divide it into doable chunks. Kendra had always regretted not getting an education, but at age 43, she wasn't about to sit through four years of high school classes. Then someone told her about the GED (graduate equivalency degree) that would take the place of her high school diploma. Within a month of passing the test—on the first try—she had signed up for classes at the local community college and was well on her way toward the long-dreamed-of education.

Don't forget to add the "silly" things to your list of goals, too. As one woman approached her seventieth birthday, she thought regretfully of all the things she had never had an opportunity to learn, particularly roller-skating. Something inside her demanded that she call the local rink to check on lessons. Though she was the oldest one in the beginners' class, and was decked out in knee and elbow pads and a helmet, she learned! And she didn't break anything in the process. Once she'd achieved that goal, she decided to tackle something else. Soon her list was rather lengthy, and she decided that she had so many fun things planned that she didn't have time to get old.

Hang on to this thought: <u>If God has placed a dream within your heart, He will help you achieve it</u>. But you <u>must take the first step toward that goal.</u>

7. Be Willing to Accept New Challenges

One of the best ways for us to grow is by tackling unfamiliar situations, uncomfortable as they may be. As I look at all the Lord has allowed to come into my life, I'm amazed at how often I've been forced to grow. For example, I had never pumped gasoline before my husband's last extended hospital stay. The day came, though, when I knew if I didn't fill the tank, I would be stranded on Michigan's I-94. The closest gas station was self-serve, so I had to plunge into unknown territory. I was concerned, though, that I wouldn't pump the gasoline correctly. What if I caused something to jam? Or worse, what if I blew up my end of town because I didn't push the buttons in the right order?

I pulled up to the tank and whispered a prayer of "Please help." (I wonder if the Lord ever chuckles at some of our prayers. Does He ever want to say, "Believe Me, this one is already solved"?) As I got out to study the pump, I saw to my great relief that the directions were written on the side: "1. Unscrew the gas cap. 2. Take the pump handle out of the holder. 3. Turn the pump switch to 'On.' 4. Insert the nozzle into the car's gas tank. 5. Squeeze."

I ought to be embarrassed to make this public confession, but I had never studied gasoline pumps. I had always been content to have the men in my life take care of those "masculine" activities. That little episode reminded me that there are many things we're afraid of in life, but when we take a deep breath and plunge on, we discover that we can get through them—and pretty well, too.

8. Take Care of Yourself

We handle life better when we're mentally and physically fit. That principle shows up in 1 Kings 19:4. It relates how God had defeated the priests of Baal in response to Elijah's prayers, by sending the fire that not only burned up the wet sacrifice, but also consumed the altar and the water in the ditch around it. But what does Elijah do after this major spiritual victory when threatened by the wicked queen? He crawls under a tree and prays to die. I love how an angel came, not to lecture him, not to remind him of everything he should be happy about, but to give him nourishment. Elijah ate and then fell asleep. Once he was fed and rested, he could listen to God. So if you're going through a tough time, nourishing food and plenty of rest is a good place to begin as you wait for the Lord's direction.

Physical activity is also a must if we are to cope well with life's challenges. Exercise not only benefits our cardiovascular system, it also releases chemicals in the brain (endorphins) that provide a sense of well-being and help us face stressful situations better. Starting an exercise program can be as easy as scheduling time for a 20-minute walk with a friend. When I worked in an office, several coworkers would climb the stairs in our building, but that was too boring for me. I like seeing trees and yards, so I tried to take a brisk walk several mornings a week. I found that even 20 minutes a day made a big difference in my energy level.

For those of you with young children, you might

think about ways to include them in your exercise routine. Linda has her young daughter ride her bike while Linda jogs alongside. Carrie runs as she pushes a sturdy stroller. Mary gives her nine-month-old daughter a handful of dry cereal after breakfast and rides her stationary bike until the child starts to fuss. Sometimes she gets in a whopping 20 minutes. Other times she "bikes" only 10 minutes. But that's 10 more minutes than she would have gotten if she hadn't bothered.

9. Spend Time with God

It's important for us to keep the lines of communication open with God. He is our oasis, our source of refreshing shade and life-giving water. Time with Him revives our spirits so that we have the strength to go out and face the world again. Try to spend a few moments each day sitting quietly with the Lord. You'll find your very spirit renewed.

Also, I've discovered that when I put my trust and security in God instead of in my circumstances, I stay anchored when storms blow into my life. For years I'd read Philippians 4:4 with the emphasis on the wrong word: I thought the verse said, "REJOICE in the Lord always. I will say it again: REJOICE!" I had a long list of experiences I couldn't get thrilled about—including several unfortunate childhood situations, rejection from my in-laws because I was "from the hills," and my husband's death from brain cancer at only 39. How could I rejoice?

But one day as I was meditating on the verse and praying about its meaning, I suddenly realized I had been reading it incorrectly, emphasizing only the rejoice part. The verse actually says, "REASON IN THE LORD always"—not in circumstances, not in people, but *in the Lord.* That little twist makes a big difference. Instead of being tossed around by the circumstances of our lives, we can find stability and joy in the knowledge that God, our Anchor, will never be separated from us.

10. Schedule Time with Your Family

Those of us who are older appreciate this truth: "At the end of life, no one has ever said, 'I wish I'd spent more time at the office.' "

I remember all too well sitting on the shore of beautiful Lake Michigan just a few months before my husband's death. As we watched our young children play in the waves, Don quietly said he wished he could call back all the times he chose to be away from us. But, of course, that was impossible.

When I was thrust into raising our children alone, I claimed Romans 12:15 as our new family verse: "Rejoice with those who rejoice; mourn with those who mourn." As our emotional healing progressed, I determined to put that verse into practice with Jay and Holly. Together and individually, I scheduled time with the children when we could share the circumstances of our day, good and bad, or just do something silly together. Those times paid off as Jay and Holly headed toward their teen years, and we were spared many of the communication problems we could have had. Even now, as Jay and

Holly are solidly into their twenties, we still enjoy the time we spend together.

11. Sprinkle Laughter into Your Day

I need an occasional chuckle so much that I bought a mug imprinted with "If You Are Too Busy to Laugh, You Are Too Busy." That's a good reminder in the midst of even the most intense day that we have to be willing to see the humor in situations. Recently, my ailing computer printer threw itself into fast mode, spewing out blank paper sheets faster than I could grab them. As I finally thought to push the "Off" button, the image of that machine having power over me, a supposedly strong and competent woman, struck me as uproariously funny, and I laughed aloud. That certainly beats grumpily complaining to everyone within earshot about "machines taking over the world."

It also helps to have friends who can lift your spirits with funny stories. One of those friends is Bob Garner, who loves retelling his North Carolina adventures as much as I love hearing them. Recently, in the midst of a glum day, I called his department to check on the details of a mutual project.

"Bob, first I need to hear some *right* talkin'," I said in my best Kentucky mountain dialect.

Without missing a beat, Bob jumped into an account of stopping for directions at an old-time general store. His guide simply told him, "Turn left or right—it won't matter—just before the bridge that was painted orange before they painted it silver."

Bob and I laughed together, then solved the problem I'd called him about. When I hung up the phone, I was smiling. And all because I recognized my need for laughter and then dared to go after it.

12. Learn to Relax

Even when laughable situations aren't readily available, we can pull encouragement into our lives by giving ourselves permission to relax. But make sure the chosen method of relaxation is one that truly produces the healing your body and mind need. Hanging out at the neighborhood pool day after day is not my idea of a good time; also, I enjoy only an occasional movie, and mindless TV doesn't capture me at all. My favorite activities include leisurely walks with friends and strolls through historical buildings where I can fill the rooms and my imagination with long-ago people who also struggled through this thing we loosely call "life."

I also try to be good to my tired shoulders with regular visits to a licensed manual therapist, who unties the muscle knots caused by lengthy hours of typing. Other people work in their gardens, listen to sounds of the shore, soak in a bubble bath, or read a good book. But whatever you choose, make sure that it truly is relaxing and doesn't become just one more thing to cross off your "to do" list.

13. Try to View Others with Compassion

The School of Hard Knocks has taught me that everyone—rich or poor, intelligent or not so intelligent, attractive or not so attractive—carries at least one great hurt. Paige was tall and beautiful—and aloof. The other girls in her dorm thought she was stuck-up as she responded to their greetings with only a nod of her head, or fielded their questions with monosyllabic answers. Gradually, they stopped talking to her. If they had been patient and had attempted to draw her out more, they would have discovered that she actually had a severe stuttering problem and didn't trust herself to say more than one or two words.

Haven't we all dismissed someone without trying to get to know who that person really was? What a great loss, both to us and to the lonely person who needed our friendship!

14. Celebrate Our Differences

This is not a perfect world, and we're not perfect people, so why not encourage ourselves with the delicious thought that it's okay for us to be different, to be who we are? To remind myself of that last point, I have on my desk a Mason pint jar filled with antique buttons—tiny pearls from a baby's gown, coarse browns from a work shirt, bright blues from a Sunday dress, and my favorite, a bold red, green, and purple button that may have "fancied up" an otherwise drab winter coat. I found the jar in an Iowa antique shop at a time when I was feeling less than perfect. Actually, the jar I bought was positioned next to one filled with white pearl buttons; but I ignored that first collection and purchased the jar filled with contrast and color—and imperfect fasteners.

Now whenever I get in one of my "I'm not good enough" moods, I need only to look at my jar of buttons to be reminded that life would be rather boring if we were all the same. A simple thought, certainly, but one that is packed with encouragement as I face the challenges of each new day.

Maybe you can identify with my occasional feelings of inadequacy. If so, listen to me: You do have great value! (Remember, the Lord loves you so much that He died for you.) *So, determine right now to be open to encouragement's power to change lives—starting with your own.* The thought that we have a responsibility to pull encouragement into our lives may be a new concept to some. But I find it comforting to know that we aren't powerless and that we don't have to wait passively for someone else to encourage us. So, what encouragement do you need? Are you willing to honestly assess your good qualities, find the positive even in difficult situations, and then set specific goals for yourself? If so, you're well on your way to the bright future we all want. If you haven't yet reached that point emotionally, the next chapter, which deals with letting go of the past, may prove helpful. I don't know about you, but I'm ready to do my part to be the woman God created me to be.

Quick Encouragement

1. Believing truly makes it so. If we think we're going to fail, we probably will.

2. Learn to take off your mask and be honest with yourself—and others.
3. Think positively and try to appreciate your good points.
4. Sometimes trying to find the positive in a difficult situation makes it easier to handle.
5. Remember the lesson from Elijah: When we are tired and hungry, we can't think clearly.
6. Spend time with God every day. Your weary spirit will be renewed.
7. Concentrate on rejoicing in the Lord, and not in circumstances or people.
8. Sprinkle laughter into your day.
9. View others with compassion. After all, our differences are what make life interesting.

Discussion Questions

1. What experience have you had that would cause you to agree or disagree with the statement "Whether you think you can or you can't, you'll be right"?
2. What can you do well?
3. What do you still want to learn or achieve? What steps do you need to fulfill that goal?
4. What challenge (such as Sandra's pumping gas) seemed scary at first?
5. How do you spend time with God each day?
6. How would you describe yourself if you were a button in a jar?

3

Letting Go of the Past

*O*n my refrigerator door is a yellowed *Peanuts* cartoon. Charlie Brown is on the pitcher's mound, and Lucy is handing him the ball.

"Sorry I missed that easy fly ball, Manager," she says. "I thought I had it, but suddenly I remembered all the others I've missed."

As she turns away in the final panel, she says, "The past got in my eyes."

Do you identify with that situation? I sure can. One morning, while playing tennis, I missed a perfect forehand, then grumbled at myself, embarrassed that I had performed poorly in front of my new partner, Iris. I missed the next shot as well. Again, I apologized.

Iris said softly, "Play the *next* ball, Sandra."

The *next* ball? Of course. I had been so intent upon

replaying that missed shot in my mind that I was missing the balls after that, too—just like Lucy.

Unfortunately, I identify with the past getting in my eyes in more areas than just sports. But in life's journey, I've learned that it is possible to let go of experiences that are keeping us from being open to encouragement. I also know that even letting go is a process as we first look at the events honestly, learn to understand their power, and then use that new understanding to move confidently into a brighter future.

Choosing to Let Go

Too many people excuse their mistakes by blaming their parents or early childhood for the way their lives have turned out. Sure, our childhood sets the precedent for the kinds of people we are as adults, but our fates aren't set in stone. At some point in the journey, we can make the decision that the unhealthy familial patterns will stop with us. Whether we get the needed encouragement to rebuild our lives through counseling or personal spiritual awareness, we do not have to cling to past trauma or pass it on to our children.

A few years ago, Karen called her parents to thank them for the early Christmas gifts they had sent. After the usual chit-chat, her dad said, "I wish you could be home for Christmas."

Scenes of earlier holidays darted through Karen's mind: her father's grumpiness if he was awakened too early, her having to beg him to open the pitiful little gifts she gave, his complaints about the relatives who stopped in. . . . Karen had long ago given up the hope of having a tension-free holiday with her family of origin, so she concentrated on her own young children and tried to create peaceful memories they would carry into their adulthood.

Thus, instead of arguing with her father over the phone lines that morning, she gently replied, "I know." Then as she watched her children playing quietly near the Christmas tree, she said to herself, *I am home.*

Much of Karen's inner peace came from having accepted, years earlier, the fact that, though her dad had not been what she had needed as a child, he had done the best he knew how. She found that emotional freedom by using some of the principles I'll outline in the next few pages and by giving up her desire to open her father's eyes to the hurtful things he had done. Determined not to pass the family pain along to her own children, she encouraged herself to grow emotionally.

For many like Karen, the holidays are filled with memories that are far from a cozy gathering around the fireplace. And when extended families do gather, tension, disappointment, and increased stress abound— and all with everyone trying to pretend nothing is wrong. Melinda knows that scenario all too well. When her birth family gets together, the results are disastrous, since her adult siblings revert to their childhood patterns in the way they react to each other and to their parents. Her only brother, even at 42, believes that his lone sonship provides him with special privileges such as insisting that his favorite dishes be prepared by their elderly mother for each meal and that his sisters follow his whims for each day's activities. Her younger sister, the one her father called "Beauty," is a buyer for a major department store chain, but under the old roof, she assumes the whining personality of the eight-year-old she used to be. Melinda's older sister, a talented professional, can't relax and becomes the controller once again as she cleans out cabinets and rearranges their mother's kitchen. Even Melinda, an award-winning teacher, again finds herself belittled by her siblings.

Why does Melinda find these actions so painful? Because she realizes she and her siblings are adults acting like children. And when she is performing the old childhood role, she is also experiencing the same feelings she felt when she was mistreated as a child. Emotionally, she has moved back into that early situation where others were pounding her self-esteem and she was convinced she was not lovable.

When old childhood roles are being played out in the lives of adults, no one appreciates the accomplishments each one has made in the passing years. Wisely, though, early in their marriage, Melinda encouraged her husband to join her in shaping their own holiday traditions. Then, throughout the year, they invite her siblings to visit separately to get to know them as adult individuals. By refusing to stay in the old role, Melinda has found a way to keep the past from getting in her eyes and marring her future.

Characteristics of Dysfunctional Families

When I worked in a New York editorial office, the staff planned an article on adult children of alcoholics (ACOA), and I was chosen to attend an ACOA convention in nearby Tarrytown. Though I don't like placing folks into pigeonholes, I was amazed at the similarities among those raised in dysfunctional homes. The most encouraging part for me was learning that if those who grew up in such families can learn to understand the patterns, they will have insight into why they react in a particular way to life's crises. That understanding, in turn, can show them a way out of old destructive behaviors.

Some of these patterns are:

- The adult Child of the Dysfunctional Family, whom I'll call a CDF, needs to know that inside is a needy person trying not to be needy. He has grown up in a house filled with fear—fear of abandonment, fear of confrontation, fear of being left out, fear of anger.

- For the CDF, control is a big issue. Since her childhood home was usually out of control, she will attempt to control any area open to her, often with endless rules and lists.

- A CDF doesn't know what "normal" is, including how relationships between family members are supposed to work.

- A CDF often makes a wonderful employee because he trusts outer direction rather than inner direction. He's always looking to someone who will show him how the system is supposed to work.

- A CDF would rather deal with the pain she knows than the pain she doesn't know. This is often seen through a CDF's being addicted to "empty wells"—partners who are emotionally unavailable.

- The CDF continues to internalize what his parents said. He doesn't process "You're stupid; get out of my sight" as the mumblings of a drunk or an emotionally unstable adult, but as a true statement about his own lack of value.
- When a CDF has children, she is determined to correct the past. "I'll do things differently," she says. "My children are going to be happy. They're going to have everything I didn't." More than one couple have applied that philosophy and produced—to their bewilderment—lazy, ungrateful children. The fact is, children are not going to be responsible if Mom and Dad keep them from responsibility.
- The CDF is often jealous of her children because they have such a great parent! She also has difficulty letting those children grow up because then she loses her childhood *again*.
- The CDF has grown up with three unspoken rules: Don't talk, don't trust, don't feel.
- Emotional freedom comes, finally, as the CDF realizes that his parents could not do any better. But that conclusion, as well as forgiveness, may take years.

Steps to Help You Let Go

The following suggestions aren't magical, and in some cases they may need to be considered under the guidance of a godly professional counselor. But if you want to let go of the past to accept encouragement's strength and a better present and future, you may want to consider them.

① Replace Old Mental Tapes with New Ones

Too often we can't give ourselves encouragement or accept it from others because we're dwelling on past injustices, believing negative things people have told us about ourselves, or rejecting the idea that we deserve anything good. Even though this first suggestion of replacing negative thoughts seems simplistic, it's a good place to start. Self-talk such as "Well, of course I failed. Why did I even try?" doesn't solve the challenge at hand; it forces our attention to the problem instead of a possible solution. Think of the difference even a simple "Well, that didn't work. What are some other possibilities?" would make in our attitude.

The following self-talk helps me to deal with tough days:

"The Lord didn't bring me this far to leave me alone."
"I can do this."
"I've survived worse."
"This, too, shall pass."
"I will not let the 'turkeys' win."

And my grandmother's "There are some things in life that all you can do with 'em is bear 'em."

Of course, none of these statements is the magic wand that makes the problem go away, but each can provide an important moment of new perspective that helps us to not give in to panic.

② Be Patient with Yourself

It took us many years to lock the negative ways of thinking into our brains, but in time we can undo that early damage. When Freda was young, her father had taken his own frustration about life out on her, telling her not to expect to achieve anything worthwhile. As an adult, Freda's way of overcoming that trauma was by keeping in her purse a list of positive thoughts she had either read or heard. She would pull the list out every time the memory of one of her father's sarcastic comments threatened her plans. A couple of years ago, she struggled with wanting to take an interior design class at the local college. Finally, she decided to go for it; but when she arrived at campus registration and saw the long line of young, attractive students, she heard her father say, "You're out of your league."

This time, instead of agreeing with that mental tape and going home, she pulled out her list and read "The past can't hold you prisoner unless you give it permission" and "The family you came from is important, but not as important as the family you will leave behind." Taking a deep breath, she took her place in line, determined to replace her fear of failure with the excitement of reaching toward a dream. That accomplishment opened the way for her to dare to reach more of her goals.

③ Learn to Forgive

One of the biggest blocks to encouragement comes when we refuse to forgive. We've all read the books and, better yet, the scriptures about forgiveness, but it can still be a difficult thing to do. However, I'm learning that freedom comes as we work *through* the situation, to where we can truly forgive another. I've lost count of the times I've reminded an angry woman that holding a grudge only hurts her, not the other person. I've even said, "He's not losing sleep over this; you are. You've got to let this go." I've never insisted—either for myself or for others—upon an immediate and flippant "Hey, it's okay you were rotten to me. No problem. Really." I stress that forgiveness is a process that we must work through.

One of my Denver friends, Dr. Linda Williams, offered the best forgiveness advice I've ever received: "Forgiveness is the willingness to live with the consequences of another's sin." I like that. Many times we can do nothing but choose to live with another's wrong actions and get on with life. Freedom comes as we make the decision to work toward forgiveness.

But what if someone doesn't acknowledge that they've hurt us, or, worse yet, hurt our child? I'm well aware Jesus said that if we get hit on one cheek, we're to turn the other as well. Yet, even as many of us mouth forgiveness outwardly, we're really seething inside. I've tried that route and found it's far better to talk out the situation immediately and not let it get lost in time.

For example, a New York friend was aggravated with me, so when my daughter, Holly, stopped by her house, the woman said, "What are you doing here?" and shut the door in her face. While Holly stood on the porch, bewildered at this uncharacteristic action on my friend's part, the woman opened the door again and said, "Are you still here?" and shut it again. Then she opened the door a third time and said, "I was just kidding. Come in."

Holly's visit was short. At dinner, she cried as she described the scene to her brother and me. I wish I had picked up the phone right then and asked for an explanation, but I thought my friend would see that as pettiness on my part. So I forced myself to talk about forgiveness with my teens and tried to dismiss it. But instead of being confronted and then forgiven, the event stuck in my craw, causing me to withdraw from the woman.

More than a year later, at a party, my friend made a sarcastic remark about my feeble photography abilities. I immediately found something to do on the other side of the room. Later, she came into the kitchen, all smiles, to invite me to her church concert. My polite decline prompted her to demand an explanation for my "bad attitude" over the previous year. When I offered the door-closing scene as an explanation, she denied it, saying there was no way she ever would have done anything like that to Holly.

Now I was truly bewildered. Holly isn't a liar, but neither is my friend. What had happened? How could I offer forgiveness for something she was insisting had never happened? I began my quest to find out. Back in Colorado Springs, I spoke with Dr. Robert Coutts and his wife, Mary, who were working in the area of neuropsychology. As we talked about brain chemistry, I learned that negative memories can be repressed to the point that a person has absolutely no recollection of them.

To illustrate the brain's power to dismiss painful memories, Dr. Coutts told me about one of his counseling sessions in which a mother called her adult son, who was also in the meeting, "the world's worst" in his particular profession. The son fretted about his mother's comment for several days and couldn't wait to discuss it at the next session. But when Dr. Coutts asked the mother about it the following week, she insisted she never would have said anything so hurtful to her son.

Fascinated by that account, I began to sympathize with the pressures my friend must have been living under to make her dismiss the door-closing scene with Holly. The incident was so important to Holly and me that we remembered it, but my friend had truly forgotten it. In scientific ways, Dr. and Mrs. Coutts reminded me that we are indeed "fearfully and wonderfully made."

Though I haven't shared any of this information with my friend, knowing about brain chemistry has helped me to forgive her actions. I realize now that she wasn't trying to deceive me by pretending the incident hadn't happened, but that, so far as her memory was concerned, it really hadn't happened. I've also decided that all future misunderstandings will get an immediate settlement with the person herself—no more of this quiet suffering in silence.

The Bible offers an example of the benefits of confronting someone directly. First Samuel 1:1–17 relates the story of Hannah and Eli. Hannah had no children—unlike her husband's other wife, Peninnah. One year, during the annual trek to the Temple, Hannah, in anguish, prayed silently, asking for a child. The priest, Eli, misunderstood and wrongly accused her of being drunk. Think about that: She was doing the *right* thing, and she was misunderstood.

When Eli accused her of drunkenness, Hannah had several choices. She could lash out at him in anger; she could tearfully slip away, crying about being wrongly accused; or she could choose a third—and correct—response: communicate directly with her accuser. She chose the latter.

To Eli's accusation, Hannah replied, "Not so, my lord . . . I am a woman who is deeply troubled. I have not been drinking wine or beer; I was pouring out my soul to the LORD" (v. 15). Eli then said, "Go in peace, and may the God of Israel grant you what you have asked of him" (v. 17). Sometime later, Hannah became pregnant.

What a wonderful example her story is. Not only is immediate communication the key to avoiding petty misunderstandings that can grow into monsters, but it may also provide a much needed blessing.

(4) Consider Additional Forgiveness

What about the times we can't accept encouragement because we won't forgive ourselves for some long-ago action? One mother couldn't forgive herself for not going to her son's wedding. A young friend of mine said she wished she had never gotten an abortion. Another friend said she should have tried harder at her marriage; it was her fault she and her husband had gotten divorced.

We can quote 1 John 1:9—"If we confess our sins, he is faithful and just and will forgive us our sins and purify us from all unrighteousness"—to ourselves until we're purple, but nothing will change if we don't take that scripture to heart. Even though it seems rather arrogant not to accept the forgiveness that our heavenly

Father offers, sometimes we need help getting out of our emotional ruts. I remember agonizing over a decision I'd made years ago. Without giving details, I mentioned my struggle to a coworker.

He listened, then picked up his mug. As he headed to the kitchenette to get coffee, he said, "Remember that you made your decision based on the information you had at the time."

He undoubtedly didn't give it another thought as he strolled toward the coffee urn, but I stood in my office doorway marveling at the relief that dropped around my shoulders like a comforting blanket.

In addition to forgiving ourselves and others, we may need to ask someone we've hurt to forgive us. I remember a call I had to make just to get peace from having hurt someone years before. I held my breath as I listened to the phone ring, almost hoping no one would be home. Then with the "Hello," I apologized, even babbled, expecting to hear a solid slamming of the receiver. I'd already decided that that would be fine; at least I would have done what I was supposed to do. But no one hung up, and we talked for more than an hour, clearing up an old misunderstanding.

That simple call in which I asked for forgiveness freed me from cringing each time I thought of that person— and provided me with a clean slate in that relationship.

(5) Surround Yourself with Supportive Friends

Emily had trouble making decisions. Even selecting a birthday card could throw her into a panic. More than once she bought two cards—one serious, one humorous—and sent them to the same individual. Most of her friends thought the action excessive and a little strange but shrugged it off. One friend, though, decided to ask her about it over lunch.

Emily hesitated but finally answered, "When I can't decide which card someone would like, I send both so they'll be happy with at least one."

Her friend nodded. "Okay," she said. "But one card is enough."

Emily frowned. "But what if you don't like the card I picked out?"

"I just think it's great when someone remembers my birthday," her friend answered. "You could send your greetings on a brown paper bag, and I'd still be thrilled."

Emily shook her head. "Boy, I wish my grandma had had that attitude. She found something wrong with every card I ever sent her."

Her friend leaned forward. "Emily," she said, "that was then, this is now. You're an adult. You don't have to keep trying to please a dead grandmother."

Emily sighed as though she had been holding her breath for a long time. And all because a supportive friend took the time to help her see reality.

6 Give Yourself a Silly Gift

My friend Marian went shopping one afternoon with her 72-year-old neighbor, Ruth. As they browsed in an antique shop, Ruth gently picked up a doll with soft curls.

"I used to have a doll just like this when I was a little

girl," she said, her eyes filling with tears. Gradually, Marian pulled the story from her:

I named my doll Hannah. And I loved her as though she were the little sister I'd always wanted. I was just learning to sew, and I was excited about the wardrobe I would make for her.

My father was a pastor of a small church, so we had very little. But it didn't matter; I had Hannah. Then one afternoon, my parents came into my room while I examined a scrap of velvet that had been in the box of material a neighbor had given my mother. The piece was just large enough to make a jacket for Hannah. . . .

I looked up at my parents. Both had a this-will-be-good-for-you look on their faces, as though they were about to give me some awful-tasting cough medicine.

Then my father told me he had visited a poor family that afternoon who had a daughter almost my age. "She's never had a doll," he said.

My heart froze.

My father continued, "So we'd like you to give her your doll—as unto the Lord."

Even before he finished the sentence, I was shaking my head. But my mother leaned forward and took Hannah out of my hands.

"Shame on you for being so selfish," she said. "You have so much."

I didn't see that I had so much. I only had Hannah.

By the time Ruth finished telling the story, tears were running down her cheeks. Marian stepped forward to hug her.

"Buy this doll for yourself," she insisted.

"What?" Ruth stammered. "Buy myself a doll? I'm too old for that nonsense."

Marian shook her head. "No you aren't. Buy the doll. Sew those clothes now that you wish you could have sewn then."

Ruth smiled and bought the doll. Sometimes she looks at it in the rocking chair in her bedroom and wonders if maybe—just maybe—it's the real Hannah.

Ruth's story shows the importance of encouraging ourselves even in seemingly silly ways. For her to work through the pain of a childhood experience, she had to be a parent to herself and give the child she once was the doll she really wanted.

Encouragement doesn't have to be a doll. Sometimes it can come in numerous colors packaged in a crayon box. Several years ago, I received a big box of crayons as a Christmas gift from my children. It was something that I had wanted ever since I was a child and had to share a box of crayons with everyone else. Some folks would dismiss that as a silly example, of course, but it's a reminder that it's okay to toss a few fun items into our responsibility-filled lives. After all, we can't encourage others if we refuse to encourage ourselves. And that often begins with a deep breath and a letting go of the past.

Again, let me emphasize that we do not have to be

bound to the past. As we go through the process of looking at previous events in our lives and understanding their power, we can move toward a brighter future and protect our children from those old destructive patterns. Sometimes that process involves learning to replace negative self-talk, forgiving ourselves as well as others, leaning on supportive friends, and being kind to ourselves. As we learn to let go of the hurtful things in our past, we are better prepared to zap future encouragement stealers. And all this can be an adventure, so let's enjoy it!

Quick Encouragement

1. Don't let the past get in your eyes. Keep playing the "next ball" rather than reliving those early mistakes or hurts.
2. Understanding the dynamics of your childhood home can free you from its power.
3. Throw out the old, negative mental tapes and replace them with new, uplifting ones.
4. As you make changes in your belief system and lifestyle, be patient with yourself. After all, it took you a long time to become the person you are.
5. Though it can be difficult, forgiving those who hurt you in the past is the first step toward freedom.
6. When agonizing over a past decision, remember that you made your decision based on the information you had at the time.
7. Surround yourself with supportive friends.
8. Give yourself permission to be kind to the child you once were.

Discussion Questions

1. What is your biggest struggle as you try to encourage yourself?
2. When are you most successful at encouraging yourself?
3. What is one encouraging thing you can do for yourself today?
4. What are your goals for erasing those discouraging mental tapes?
5. What "silly" or even "childish" item do you occasionally long for? How have you resolved that longing?
6. What struggle do you have with forgiveness— either toward another or toward yourself?

Zapping
the
Encouragement
Stealers

*D*eana felt like skipping as she left the community theater. The parts were posted, and she had been assigned a supporting role. When she first heard about the new theater group, she remembered the fun she'd had in her high school plays. Still, it had taken days for her to work up the courage to try out last weekend. And now, she had a major part! She couldn't wait to tell her roommates. She hadn't told them she was trying out because she didn't want them to be disappointed for her if she didn't make it. Boy, would they be surprised!

Actually, Deana was the one who was surprised. When she burst through the door with her good news, her roommates reluctantly turned from the TV to stare at her.

Finally, one said, "Gee, we never see you as it is."

The other one nodded, then added, "You'll start hanging out with your new artsy pals."

Deana started to apologize and reassure them she was still their best friend. But as she glanced at the TV, she realized she wanted her evenings to be filled with more than chocolate-covered ice cream and sitcoms.

Smiling, she said, "Well, I'm excited about the part, and I hope you'll come. We open in six weeks."

Good for Deana! She refused to allow her room-mates' attitude, and lack of encouragement, to steal her excitement. Without meaning to (I hope), her room-mates would have restricted Deana's activities—and even life—to those patterns they were comfortable with. But an encouragement stealer doesn't have to be a person. Many times it can be an attitude, as we behave in a way that steals our own encouragement. In the following pages, we'll look at some encouragement stealers and consider ways we can lessen their power.

Ways to Zap the Encouragement Stealers

1) Rely on the Scriptures

In 1981, Carolyn was determined to study medicine and had the good grades to support such a decision. Unfortunately, her favorite uncle insisted that women are more suited to nursing and that she should do herself a favor and get "doctoring" out of her head. Bewildered, she asked his reason and was astonished to hear that women were created to be a husband's "helpmeet" and were not designed for leadership roles. She literally bit her tongue to keep from saying the harsh words that sprang to her mind. Instead of arguing, she turned to the Scriptures and gathered examples of godly women—such as Deborah, the Old Testament judge—who were in leadership roles. She never convinced her uncle that she had God's blessing upon her chosen profession, but at least she was convinced within her own mind. Today, she has a thriving family practice in Minnesota and is grateful she ran her long-ago decision through the Scriptures' filter.

2) Realize You Can't Please Everyone

My favorite Aesop fable sums up this point perfectly: A father and his son were on their way to market, leading their donkey and enjoying the beautiful morning together.

One of their neighbors saw them and said, "Now isn't that silly? You have a fine donkey, but both of you are walking."

So the father set his son on the donkey, and they continued toward the market.

But after a few minutes, another neighbor saw them and said to the son, "How rude you are to ride while your old father must walk."

So the child hopped off the donkey's back, the father climbed on, and they continued their journey.

Within a few minutes they were met by yet another neighbor, who glared at the father and said, "What kind of father are you that you make this child walk while you, a grown man, ride?"

So the father pulled his son up to sit in front of him

on the donkey's back. It wasn't long, though, until they passed a fourth neighbor.

"How thoughtless you are," he said, "to make this poor donkey carry both of you to town."

So they slid off the donkey, and the father promptly picked up the animal and effortlessly put it across his shoulders.

As they walked along, another neighbor saw them. "Well, that is the most stupid thing I've ever seen—a donkey being carried."

The obvious moral is that we can't please everyone. And as soon as we try, we'll run into encouragement stealers at every turn.

3) Don't Expect Others to Appreciate Your Efforts

In 1968, my husband, Don, and I drove to Kentucky to take my grandparents, Papa and Mama Farley, and my aunt Adah to Michigan. An eight-hour return drive was ahead of us, so my grandmother had a large lunch basket perched next to her on the front seat. On top of the basket she placed a bunch of bananas, then settled her cane comfortably against her thigh, ready for the trip.

In the late 1960s, Interstate 75 wasn't complete yet, and numerous detours forced us over the old, hilly roads. Topping one more hill, we discovered that a rock slide had covered the asphalt. Don got out of the car after hastily throwing the gear of the still-running vehicle into park. Then, just as he climbed onto the rock pile to survey the situation, the car stalled and began to roll backward.

I was in the backseat between Aunt Adah and Papa, but it was up to me to reach the brake. In an instant, I threw myself over the seat, knocking the lunch to the floor as I scrambled to stomp on the brake. When I got the car stopped, it was already several feet off the pavement on the side of the road. And beyond that was a 500-foot drop into the ravine below.

With the car safely braked again, I released my breath and then looked at Mama Farley. Surely she had some praise for the quick action on my part that had saved the four of us from severe injury—if not death.

But she was picking up the lunch. "You smashed the bananas," was her only comment. So much for my need to have my efforts recognized.

4) Don't Give Others
    Power Over You

We allow others to become encouragement stealers when we give them control over how we feel about ourselves. Former prisoners of war often report that they were determined not to let their captors dictate their emotions. Thus, if the guard was in a bad mood, the prisoner forced himself to be cheerful. And if the guard was in a jovial mood, the prisoner would be aloof.

We may nod as we read that, understanding the importance of not letting an enemy control our emotions even though he controls our physical conditions, but most of us *do* absorb the reactions we receive from others. I remember an account from several years ago in which a famous concert pianist was giving a performance before 3,000 people. At the end, the audience was on its feet, clapping and calling, "Bravo!" The pianist took his bow, but his eyes were on the lone occupant of the box seat on the first tier. That man remained seated. Suddenly, the pianist turned and strode off stage, refusing to come back for an encore.

Later, a friend who had witnessed the abrupt exit asked him about it. "You had 3,000 people on their feet shouting your praises," he said. "But you ignored them and looked only at that one man. Why?"

The pianist quietly replied, "The man was my teacher!"

Too many of us can identify with that story, but we need to remember that we do have control over how we react to situations and that we do not have to be bound by yet another encouragement stealer. We can choose to look to the 3,000 or to the lone occupant who we believe has power over us.

5) Don't Let Life's Little Trials Upset You

Ever notice that when we're complaining, we're like those who are served a tasty trout but allow two overlooked bones to ruin the entire meal? I'm chief among sinners in this area, especially since I become easily aggravated over perceived injustices in the rush of daily life.

Recently, I picked up a little gesture that really helps my attitude: I turn my hands palms down to remind myself that whatever the latest irritation is, it certainly isn't worth my tension. Turning my palms downward is my way of saying, "Let it go, Sandra. Let it go." Then as

I turn my palms up again, I'm saying to the Lord, "Fill my hands with what You want me to have."

I confess that I don't always turn my palms down in a gentle fashion. Sometimes I thrust them toward the floor so quickly that it seems as if my hands will snap right off. But the gesture helps.

6) Don't Let Worry Weigh You Down

We also can't encourage anyone if we're bound by worry. First Peter 5:7 says, "Cast all your anxiety on him because he cares for you." But this isn't a glib statement of "Just give it to the Lord, honey." Giving up something that we've carried for a while can be difficult for many of us, especially if we're prone to take it back two minutes after we've prayed about it and supposedly released it. But this, too, is a process. Some days we may say 9,847 times, "Okay, Lord, here's that big worry." But the next day we may have to give it up only 5,682 times. And the day after that only 2,756 times. Eventually, as we practice letting go, we will get to the place where we say, "Here, Lord," and mean it for the entire day.

For those folks who need something tangible to do with their worries, here are a couple of suggestions:

1. *Place your concerns in mental boxes.* One woman pretended to place the fretful situation into a mental box. Then, still in her mind, she wrapped that box, put a big bow on it, and placed it on the closet shelf. Every time she'd find herself worrying about that particular problem, she'd force herself through the mental exercise

of taking the box off the shelf, undoing the bow, unwrapping the box, and pulling out the worry. It was such a mental ordeal that she finally decided the problem wasn't worth the effort of worrying about it.

*2. *Collect your daily concerns in a God Bag.* For those of you who don't like mental exercises, you may be happier with an actual "God Bag." One of my friends writes "God Bag" on the outside of a brown lunch sack. Then every time he worries, he writes the concern on a scrap of paper and drops it into the bag. Once a month, he'll go through the paper slips and see how God has answered him. As you place each worry in your God Bag, you're reminding the Lord—and yourself—that you trust Him to answer in His time and in His way.

One thing I want to emphasize: I don't offer any of this lightly because I understand worry all too well. Recently, I struggled over the whole biblical concept of "Fear not" as Holly had a suspicious mole removed from her hand. Because of the family history of malignant melanoma, waiting for the biopsy report would have been grueling enough. But the waiting was compounded by concern over unexpected car repair bills; Jay's wrestling over whether to get a job or attend graduate school; my aging parents' failing health; and a friend's work dilemma that seemed to be forcing an out-of-state move. And I— the doer—could do nothing but wait. And pray. And concentrate on being in God's presence. When Holly's lab report came back "Negative, but bears watching for future changes," I was grateful for both the reprieve and the Lord's scriptural reminders of His presence, such as Philippians 4:6: "Do not be anxious about anything, but in everything, by prayer and petition, with thanksgiving, present your requests to God." I can't control all the crises that are part of life, but I can trust Him to guide me through them. And sometimes that's the only peace in times of worry and stress.

Quick Encouragement

1. When others insist you are supposed to act in a certain way, use the Scriptures as your authority.
2. Realize you can't please everyone.
3. Don't expect others to appreciate everything you do.
4. Like the pianist in the story, too often we *choose* to listen to encouragement stealers.
5. We can't encourage if we're complaining.
6. Encouragement and worry can't dwell in the same thought, so don't let worry weigh you down.

Discussion Questions

1. Describe a situation in which you allowed someone to determine how you were feeling.
2. Have others ever insisted you act in a certain way? How did you handle the criticism?
3. How has your attitude—good or bad—affected how you handled a particular situation?
4. Have you ever found yourself trying to please everyone? What was the result?
5. Over the years, what have you learned about worry?

Getting a
Fresh
Perspective:
A Personal
Journey

*O*nce when my children and I were vacationing yet again in my beloved Kentucky, my son, Jay, looked up from his book and, glancing at the sycamore trees hanging over the muddy Cumberland River, asked, "Mom, what is it with you and this place?"

Quietly, I answered, "When I was a child, I was safe here."

"Well, that'll do it," he replied and turned back to his book.

Several years later, in September 1992, I needed that emotional safety again. Two years before, I had moved myself and my two children from New York to Colorado, and I was still second-guessing that decision. I was so devoid of encouragement that I felt as though I were standing in an emotional valley. I desperately needed reassurance that I hadn't missed God's direction, and I saw no option other than to get a dose of encouragement from my place of birth. With the gracious permission of my bosses, I headed to Kentucky for 12 wonderful days.

I began my trip in Ashland, a major city in Kentucky's industrialized northern section, with one of my favorite cousins, Representative Donald B. Farley. He was running for (and later won) reelection to the Commonwealth House for the 100th District. Hearing folks detail their concerns about layoffs and crime directly to their representative gave me a new appreciation for the legislative process—and for my gentle-spirited cousin with whom I shared so many memories.

After those eye-opening days, I disappeared into the southeastern coal area, in the heart of the Appalachian Mountains, where I had been born. For the first few days, I stayed at Cherry Orchard, the weekend cabin of another dear cousin, Lonnie Dunn, and found comfort in the lack of radios, TVs, and ringing phones. As I washed dishes, I listened to the sounds of animals and birds in the woods—sounds that generations of Kentucky women before me had heard.

Lonnie's hideaway is adjacent to the farm once owned by John T. Dunn, my great-grandfather, so my dad drove down from Michigan to give me a dose of family history. In the evenings, as we sat on the porch and listened to the whippoorwills, Dad told stories of the strong community of his childhood that stood together against floods, failed crops, and epidemics.

Sunday morning, we attended the "Preaching and Dinner on the Grounds" at the cemetery. Wooden folding chairs were set up on top of the hill, under the pines. Gradually, the people gathered, greeting one another and asking about absent kin. The service began with "Amazing Grace," sung in a slow, twangy way, followed by the more peppy "Now Let Us Have a Little Talk with Jesus," complete with resounding bass. The next song, "When the Roll Is Called Up Yonder," was the signal for the worshipers to leave their chairs and greet one another. By the second stanza, the women were hugging and crying—and everyone was ready for the sermon.

Tall, rugged Preacher Howard then strode to the lectern and announced, "We meet in the cemetery as a reminder that we're all gonna die and meet the Man who hung between two thieves to save us."

He started "preaching hard," his words punctuated by the women's "Amens" as they glanced toward their men swapping stories at the side of the cemetery. The children played tag near the old stones that marked the graves of my ancestors and chased each other toward the plywood tables that would soon be spread with the finest in country cooking.

The rule of most Kentucky cooks seems to be "Honey, I'd rather have a bushel too much than a teaspoon not enough," so at the closing hymn, the overflowing picnic baskets were opened, and we filled our plates with the abundance from hillside gardens and country henhouses. Meandering between clusters of friends balancing meals on the top of gravestones, we traded family gossip and pondered the upcoming winter. I felt some of my emotional strength returning.

Before I left the homestead the next morning, Dad

and I visited the nearby consolidated elementary school, where 80 percent of the children are on the free lunch program. The principal explained that families from the northern cities return to the mountains in bad economic times, swelling the school's already overburdened budget. I thought about the economic crisis that had sent our own family north in 1951, altering our lives forever. As I headed my rental car deeper into the mountains, I pondered how my life might have turned out if we hadn't been forced to leave this state. But looking at old regrets wasn't helping me deal with new disappointment, so I turned my thoughts to what I would find at my next stop.

Years ago, my maternal grandfather, Papa Farley, had been part of a quartet that participated in the contests held at the Red Bird Mission in Beverly, Kentucky. So as I planned this trip, I had called there and connected with Craig Dial, the resource development director, who, with his wife, Karen, welcomed me for what they graciously called "personal renewal." At that time, Craig and his family had been in the mountain mission for five years. The Community Store, which served as both a second-hand shop and an emergency supplier, had handled within the previous year 542 emergencies that included families hit with devastating illness, floods, or fires.

Every morning at the mission, I breathed deeply of the mountain air that had filled my lungs as a child, but as much as I needed my mountains, I needed Karen's quiet encouragement and Craig's counsel more. Even now, I smile as I remember his comment that many of us get to the end of our path, look around, wonder where God is, and throw our hands up in panic. But if we'd just look behind us, we'd realize He was still with us and that we had merely run ahead of Him. By the end of my visit, my spiritual lungs were as well filled as my physical ones.

The morning I reluctantly left Red Bird, I had planned to go to my birthplace in Harlan County, across treacherous Pine Mountain. But I was tired and needed some place to sort through the experiences of the previous days. Thus, I headed to Berea, a city near Lexington, where I could rest. I knew the area well. In the 1930s, my father had attended Berea College—an institution that has educated poor young people from the Appalachian Mountains since before the War Between the States. (Remember, Southerners insist "there's no such thing as a Civil War.")

After resting for a day at the hotel, my strength returned, and I wandered through a nearby gift shop, where I discovered several cloth dolls. I recognized the material from which their dresses were made—feed sacks! During the Depression, thrifty farm wives had made undergarments, nightgowns, and aprons from the muslin sacks, so some enterprising marketing genius came up with the idea to make the cloth sacks out of brightly colored material and charge a few extra cents. In our own farm days, my mother could make a dress for me from one sack.

Those memories came in a rush as I reached for the doll dressed in a white and purple feed sack, covered by an old tea-towel apron embroidered with purple and blue flowers. Attached to the cloth hand was a wicker basket filled with little pieces of homemade lye soap, such as we used to make on our long-ago farm. The tears were already starting as I read the accompanying handwritten card:

Cameron Leah Irvin is No. 122 in this series. When Daniel Boone cut a pass through the Cumberland Gap, Cammie's grandfather Irvin was with him. She comes from a long line of proud, resourceful mountain women.

She learned early to make soap from lye and hog fat, and quilts from any tiny bit of fabric left over from sewing.

She knows how to make beans and corn bread take the place of meat when there is no meat to be had.

She grew up hearing from her mama that mountain women are smart, loving, strong, and beautiful—and so she became just that. [I had to fight sobs at the simple description of encourage-ment's power.] I hope you enjoy her; she's quite a lady.

Her basket is full of real mountain-made soap. Her blouse was a 1930s feed sack, her apron a 1940s tea towel, and her bonnet a late-1940s dresser scarf.

I swiped at my eyes, then reached for a second doll, which was clothed in a plain muslin dress covered with a brown-and-yellow-flowered apron, the pocket of which held tiny pinecones, quartz pebbles, and even a piece of shiny coal. In her cloth hand was a three-inch grapevine wreath. That handwritten card read:

> Jeri Deanna Bargo is No. 124 in this series. Jeri D., as her friends call her, grew up in the mountains, then went to the city to live.
>
> She loves the city—she truly does—but every little while there comes up in her a heart hunger to get to the country again. [Just as I had done!] That's when she puts on her feed-sack apron with the roomy pocket and the handmade shawl and takes off on country roads. Her aim is to renew her soul with the quiet and gather a bit of the real world to take back to the city.
>
> Today she made a wreath and filled her pocket full of treasures. Her bonnet and apron were a 1930s feed sack; her shawl a 1950s doily. The lace at her neck is from the 1800s, as is her button brooch.

Both cards were signed "Designed and Created by Wanda Chapman."

Tears were running down my cheeks while the clerks mouthed "We just sold another doll" to each other. Actually, I bought both dolls.

Next, I was determined to find out if there really was a Wanda Chapman. After a few phone calls, I found her in Cumberland, Kentucky, just 20 miles from where I'd been born. When I asked about her dolls, Wanda described the closing of the mines that had put her husband out of work. As the bills stacked up, she wandered through their home, praying as she looked for something of value to sell. All she found was a pile of feed sacks.

"Lord, what can I do with this old material right now?" she asked. "I don't have enough time to make a quilt."

Suddenly, she envisioned dolls, each with its own story. Excitedly, she grabbed the material and scissors and produced dozens of dolls based on the strong women she had known over the years. Today, her Out-of-the-Attic dolls are sold all over the United States, an example of what one mountain woman can do when her back is against the wall and she's trusting the Lord to give her a new perspective about how to solve a problem.

So I, another mountain woman, went back to Colorado Springs, encouraged that while plenty of challenges were still ahead, I could face them—with the Lord.

Is there some place you need to go to get an encouraging perspective? It doesn't have to be back to your place of birth or even out of town. It just needs to be where you can reconnect with the Lord and with what is important to you—whether it's touching family heritage or making a difference in another's life. For Judy, that meant volunteering as the "Game Lady" in the children's ward at the local hospital. Mildred works in the Salvation Army soup kitchen. I remember one woman who learned sign language so she could communicate with her new neighbors' teen daughter.

Look around. What will give you that fresh perspective? We can't help it if we fall into a mud puddle, but we have only ourselves to blame if we keep sitting there. Our losses in life—whether through death, divorce, or major disappointment—may be amputations, but they don't always have to bleed. And many times how long they bleed is up to us. Remember, we may never get *over* a trauma, but we can get *through* it—by hanging on to the Lord and absorbing the strength He pours into us as we ask. In the following chapters, we'll look at some additional ways to face those inevitable crises.

Quick Encouragement

1. Looking at old regrets doesn't help us deal with new disappointment.
2. Many times, if we'd just look behind us, we'd realize that God is still with us and that we've merely run ahead of Him.
3. "She grew up hearing from her mama that mountain women are smart, loving, strong, and beautiful—and so she became just that."
4. Give yourself a fresh perspective, either through a cherished setting or by helping others.
5. Find that place where you can get an encouraging perspective by reconnecting with the Lord and with what is important to you.
6. When we fall into one of life's "mud puddles," we have only ourselves to blame if we keep sitting in it.

7. Our losses in life—whether through death, divorce, or major disappointment—may be amputations, but they don't always have to bleed.

8. We may never get *over* a trauma, but we can get *through* it—by hanging on to the Lord and absorbing the strength He pours into us as we ask.

Discussion Questions

1. Do you have a special place where you felt safe as a child? Describe it.

2. Have you ever been in a position where nothing seemed to help except a fresh perspective? What was the situation?

3. Have you ever given yourself an encouraging perspective? What was the outcome?

4. Has a simple comment from another provided special encouragement? How did it help?

5. What is one of life's "mud puddles" that you've pulled yourself out of? What or who helped give you the right perspective?

When We
Think
Life Is
Over

W hen my 22-year-old Grandpa Ted was killed in a coal mine accident, he left a young wife and three children—a three-year-old daughter (Aunt Reva), a two-year-old son (my dad), and a six-week-old baby (Uncle Ishmael). In one awful moment, Grandma Katie lost her husband, her children's father, a home, and financial security. After the funeral, she did what women often do in the South when faced with a loss: She took to her bed. Relatives and neighborhood women tried to take care of her and the children, but they were expecting her to die, too. They'd seen other grief-stricken women "pine away" under similar circumstances.

One morning, though, her father, big John T. Dunn, strode into the bedroom and said, "Katie, if you die, who's gonna take care of these young'ns?"

Her eyes widened as the thought settled that she did, indeed, still have her children. Suddenly, she threw back the quilts and put out her arms to take the baby from her neighbor; then she called the two toddlers to her side. Her father went back to the field, knowing his daughter had made a good choice and would be just fine.

Like Grandma Katie, we have choices we can make, even when we think life is over. We have more control over situations than we realize, even if it is nothing more than choosing how we will cope with them. As I said in the previous chapter, we may never get *over* a trauma, but we can get *through* it. In this chapter, we'll look at some of the practical things we can do to open our thought processes to encouragement's power.

Starting the Process

① Acknowledge the Crisis

When remembering a hurtful situation, often the last thing we want to do is relive the details. We'd much rather push them aside. But if we don't look at the crisis, we won't be able to deal with it; and if we don't deal with it, we'll never be free from it.

For years, Tammy refused to talk about her father's death, saying that it was something that happened a long time ago. But when her own daughter turned 12— the age Tammy had been when her father died— Tammy became irritable and overly protective, even rescinding privileges, such as sleep-overs, that she had readily granted before. It was only when her mother mentioned the age similarities that Tammy realized how young she had been to have endured such a loss. Once she acknowledged the pain, she allowed herself to grieve it and thus be healed from it.

② Give Yourself Permission to Grieve

A few months after my husband died, an acquaintance whom I'll call Rachel approached me one Sunday morning after the service. As she hugged me, she said, "I must tell you what an inspiration you've been to me as I've watched you adjust to widowhood. I'm so impressed that you never cried after Don died. What faith!"

I stared at her for a few moments, struggling with how to answer. To let her continue to think that I hadn't cried was a lie. But would the truth make her think less of me? Finally, I shook my head. "I'm sorry to disappoint you, Rachel," I said. "But I *did* cry after Don died. In fact, I even screamed a few times. It's just that you never *saw* me cry."

She looked startled, but I continued. "I wish life's griefs would stop with me. They won't, though. And when your turn comes, you need to know that it's okay to cry even as you lean on the Lord. He understands tears."

I knew Rachel was disappointed, but I couldn't leave her thinking that good Christians are always dry-eyed. That would have been dishonest on my part and would have set her up for unhealthy future grief. We need to look to Jesus as our perfect example of how to handle sorrow. He lamented over Jerusalem (Matthew 23:37; Luke 13:34), wept at the tomb of Lazarus (John 11:35),

and fell anguished to the ground in the Garden of Geth-
semane (Matthew 26:39; Mark 14:35). So when we hit
the low points in our lives, we need to remind ourselves
that it's okay to cry.

And if you're the one watching a friend go through a
painful time, I trust you won't flippantly quote Romans
8:28 and go on your way. Romans 8:28 *is* true, but I
need to quote it to myself when I'm hurting, not hear it
mouthed by some well-meaning, nonhurting friend. Just
wrap that sorrowing person in a big hug and cry with
her. God gave us tear ducts for a reason.

Actually, when we're under stress, crying is a healthy
thing for us to do. In the early 1980s, William H. Frey II,
Ph.D., director of the Alzheimer's Research Laborato-
ries at Regions Hospital in St. Paul, Minnesota, led a
team of researchers testing the content of tears. By
comparing the tears shed when the subjects peeled
onions against the tears shed when those same people
watched a sad movie, the researchers discovered noticeable chemical differences.[1]

Dr. Frey further found that 85 percent of women
and 73 percent of men say they "feel better" after
crying. That's enough for me to be convinced that the
tears caused by emotional stress are releasing a chemical that would cause further problems—ranging from
headaches to severe physical illness—if allowed to
continue to build up.

Rachel herself, soon after our talk at church, had an
opportunity to give honest tears to the Lord: Her daughter and son-in-law had been trying to have a baby for
years, and they were thrilled when their pregnancy went

full term. But in the final week, the baby suddenly went into fetal distress and was delivered stillborn. If the grandmother had still been caught in the misunderstanding that faith keeps us from tears, she would not have been able to hug her daughter and cry with her.

③ Work Through Your Guilt

When I was part of a Michigan grief counseling team a decade ago, I learned that guilt comes in three shapes: true, false, and misplaced. *True guilt* results from our wrong action. The only way to get rid of that is by confessing it—first to the Lord and then to the person we've wronged—and asking for forgiveness. And for those people from whom we can't ask forgiveness because they're no longer part of our lives, we can still ask through an unsent letter or, if the person has died, through prayer, as we ask the Lord to pass along our message.

False guilt produces conversations filled with "I should have," as though everything bad that happens is somehow our fault: "I should have known the cancer was back." "I should have been home for her phone call." False guilt is such a common reaction to life's crises that grief counselors have a favorite story:

> A hospital chaplain visited two Michigan sons whose mothers had died in his hospital at the end of February. The first son blamed himself, saying, "My mother's death is all my fault. I should have sent her to Florida for the winter. Instead she stayed here, and the gloomy days

and harsh weather wore down her immune system. It's all my fault."

A few hours later, the chaplain met with the son of the second woman who had died. That son blamed himself, saying, "My mother's death is all my fault. I insisted upon sending her to Florida for the winter. The change in the water and the strange food wore down her immune system. It's all my fault."

Two sons, two different situations, but the same false guilt.

Misplaced guilt results when an occurrence gets blown out of proportion as the consequence of an otherwise normal activity. For example, we can send our youngster to the corner store every day for three weeks and not think anything about it. But if he gets hit by a car, we say, "I shouldn't have let him go by himself. It's all my fault!" No, it's not your fault. It was the fault of the speeding driver.

All three types of guilt can be readily used by the enemy to keep us defeated. That's why we must keep talking to the Lord, asking for His forgiveness when we've sinned, and allowing Him to encourage us so that we can go forward in His strength.

(4) Realize That Your Suffering Is Not Unique

When we hurt, we often are convinced that no one has ever suffered like this before. But pain—whether it's physical or emotional—is universal. The Chattanooga

Museum contains a letter written by a Confederate soldier in which he said, "Some of us are young, some of us are old, some of us are poor, some of us are rich, but we all bleed the same." Understanding that suffering, at one time or another, is a common experience for all of us should help us to be more compassionate to those who are hurting. Our understanding and encouragement can lessen their emotional pain. Besides, they may be hurting now, but our turn is coming.

And since we all hurt at one time or another, what if we tried to see everything we do in the light of eternity? Whenever I have an important decision to make, I do the usual things—pray, read the Scriptures, and seek godly, encouraging counsel. Then I take a walk in the local cemetery. As I read the dates and inscriptions on the gravestones, especially the old ones, I realize I'm walking an emotional path others have walked and that the only decisions that really matter are the ones that affect eternity. Knowing that I'm not the first, nor the last, to face major decisions helps, and I'm encouraged by knowing that my dilemma is not unique.

⑤ Surround Yourself with Loving and Supportive People

Sometimes we're hurting so much that we can't do any of the suggestions given above. At those times, we need a good friend who will allow us to hurt. When I first heard about the Jewish concept of "sitting shiva" with someone who is grieving, I thought of my friends who had quietly sat with me after my husband died. Then a few years ago, after I was denied a promotion for which I had moved to Colorado, I learned that encouragement can be offered in the midst of disappointment, too. That evening, while I cried, my friend Bobbie Valentine sat with me, occasionally reading psalms that verbalized my hurt, but mainly listening and quietly waiting. I'm sure it was a tough evening for her, but grieving under the watchful eye of a dear friend moved me that much faster into emotional healing.

⑥ Reach Out to Other Hurting Folks

After Don died, the children and I were constantly reminded of our loss by the sight of all the "whole" families around us. To help minimize our hurt, we decided that we would spend our holidays at the Salvation Army, serving meals to those in worse straits than ourselves: transient workers, the homeless, families caught in life's hiccups, and single-parent families. Encouraging others less fortunate than ourselves got us through the early years of our grief and set a pattern of giving that we continue today.

Don't hesitate to help someone because you don't think you're "perfect" enough. One of my favorite counselor friends, Lon Adams, is paralyzed from the waist down because of a spinal tumor. After visiting a friend at the hospital, Lon noticed a man in his early forties studying his wheelchair as they waited for the elevator.

"May I help you?" Lon asked.

The man's story tumbled out. His 16-year-old daughter had recently been paralyzed in an automobile accident and would spend the rest of her life in a wheelchair. Would Lon visit her in the hospital and encourage her that life wasn't over?

A few minutes later, Lon wheeled up to the bed of a beautiful young girl who would never again race after a soccer ball or run to class. He answered the family's questions about paralysis, listed things he could still do, and prayed with them.

Yet later he told me he wasn't sure how much help he'd been to her *sitting* in a wheelchair.

"That's the whole point," I said. "If I'm ever paralyzed, I want to hear from someone like you, not some able-bodied person telling me it's going to be all right."

While Lon saw his paralysis as a great weakness that limited his power, the newly paralyzed teen was encouraged that her life could still hold good things. And that provided enormous encouragement during a bleak time for her and her family.

⑦ Make Changes in Your Lifestyle

We all know folks who move, dye their hair, or lose weight to proclaim a new start. But the symbol doesn't have to be so dramatic. My home decorating "statement" as a single parent has long been quilts hanging on the walls, left over from the days when I couldn't afford wallpaper after moving my family to New York to start a new career in editing. Three homemade quilts still adorn the walls of my home office, a delightful contrast to the professionally decorated walls of my past. For Karen, a new start meant getting rid of the dark-colored towels her husband had insisted upon and purchasing white, peach, and cream ones. When Kim's boyfriend took a job 1,000 miles away without telling her, she worked through her depression by replacing the dark paneling in her den with bright, flowery wallpaper. All of these changes, simple though they are, represent a subtle declaration that important adjustments are taking place within the decorator's lifestyle.

⑧ Realize That Heaven Is Not on Earth

It's taken me a long time to grasp the reality that heaven isn't anywhere on this planet—not in New York, not in Colorado, and not even in Kentucky. As long as we keep looking for the perfect home, the perfect family, the perfect job, the perfect friends, we're going to keep being disappointed. How much better if we understood that we are here on this pitiful earth for only a short time and that we need to do our best to serve the Lord by serving our fellowman, I'm convinced that the "heart longing" we often feel within ourselves is actually a long-ing for our Father and heaven, and it will not be satisfied until we finally step on that celestial shore. Until we arrive there, we are to be content to do God's bidding here. Kermit Brown, a dear older member of my child-hood church, used to say as his health failed that he was "ready to go but content to stay." That is a good goal for all of us.

We can dwell on the bitter parts of our lives and become bitter ourselves, or we can concentrate on the good things and march into a brighter future. When

Allison went through an ugly divorce, she chose to dwell on the two good things that had come from that rocky marriage—her children—rather than on the activities of her former husband. And that concentration allowed her not only to dwell on the future she wanted the three of them to have, but also to work at the tangible ways she could help achieve it.

(9) Trust in God's Sovereignty

It calms me to know that God is in charge, and I am strengthened by the encouragement in such verses as Isaiah 41:9–10: "I took you from the ends of the earth, from its farthest corners I called you. [Harlan County, Kentucky, certainly qualifies!] I said, `You are my servant'; I have chosen you and have not rejected you. So do not fear, for I am with you; do not be dismayed, for I am your God. I will strengthen you and help you; I will uphold you with my righteous right hand."

I may not like how things are going, but I do like knowing that once I've given the situation to our sovereign Lord, the final outcome is in His hands. Then during those all-too-frequent times when theology doesn't explain the ongoing hurt, I'm back to Mama Farley's "There are some things in life that all we can do with 'em is bear 'em."

Many folks find peace in the Serenity Prayer: "God grant me the Serenity to accept the things I cannot change, the Courage to change the things I can—and the Wisdom to know the difference."

Rest is implied in those few words, which is exactly what we need when we've hit a situation where we think life is over. But with the Lord's help, that is not an impossible goal.

◆〈XXX〉◆

I like the old saying "Pray as though everything depends on God, and work as though everything depends on you." Just as Grandma Katie, at the beginning of this chapter, had to choose to rejoin life, we often have to make necessary choices, too. Some of those right decisions include facing emotional pain, working through any guilt, recognizing the universality of suffering, surrounding ourselves with encouraging people, and reaching out to others who are hurting. As we grasp those concepts, we have started the process that will open our weary spirits to the healing power of encouragement—not only from ourselves and other people, but also from God.

Quick Encouragement

1. We have more control over a situation than we think, even if it is nothing more than choosing how we will face it.
2. We may never get *over* a trauma, but we can get *through* it—by hanging on to the Lord and pulling out some of the God-given power within us.
3. Look to Jesus as your example in suffering. (In other words, it's okay to cry!)
4. Discover the power in friendship.
5. Find ways to reach out to other hurting folks.
6. Remember, heaven is not here on earth.

7. Rest in God's sovereignty and allow Him to encourage you.

Discussion Questions

1. What is the most difficult situation you've ever faced?
2. What helped you the most as you worked through it?
3. Has anyone ever encouraged you by "sitting shiva"? If so, how?
4. What advice would you have for someone trying to help another person?
5. Have friends ever gotten you through a difficult time? Explain.
6. Has anything good come from your pain? Explain.

Notes

1. William H. Frey II and Muriel Langseth, *Crying: The Mystery of Tears* (San Francisco: Harper, 1985).

7

Receiving
Encouragement
from
GOD

*O*ne of my most encouraging childhood memories is of my Kentucky grandparents, Papa and Mama Farley, kneeling by their living room chairs each evening and praying aloud. I'd try to pray, too, but I was so intrigued by the thought of God sorting out our voices that I never got through my own requests.

Meanwhile, I could hear the old mantel clock ticking quietly, as it had during the influenza epidemic of the early 1900s and World War I. I listened to the same ticking Mama heard in the Great Depression, when she knew that the only thing standing between her large family and hunger was the hillside garden. The clock had ticked throughout World War II when they knelt on behalf of four sons and three sons-in-law stationed in places with unpronounceable names. And it ticked through the 1950s when their children moved away from the cloistered community and to the industrial North.

I think of that little clock whenever the great "what-ifs" loom: What if something happens to my children? What if my health fails, and I can't watch them grow up? What if . . . ?

The Lord doesn't promise that we won't have trials—just as Papa and Mama Farley weren't spared all that the little clock ticked through—but we can face our problems calmly, knowing that God is with us. Often He lets us know of His presence through His special encouraging touch, but even as we grow spiritually, it may take us a while to recognize Him in the midst of a challenge.

Giving the Knots to God

As I think of the spiritual growth that we as Christians must go through, I think of the physical progress my children have made. Often the similarities make me cringe. When Holly was a toddler, her favorite expression was "Me do!" It didn't matter if she wanted to pour her own cereal, get dressed, or tie her shoes; she had to be in charge. Of course I should have been glad she was determined to be independent, but she wasn't old enough to have fine-tuned the needed skills. She'd spill the cereal—hardly my favorite sight when we were in a hurry—put her little blouse on backward, and get her laces so tangled that I'd have to work a fork prong through the knots to untie them one by one. I'll say this for Holly, though. When she'd gotten her shoelaces hopelessly tangled, she'd hand me the shoe and say, "*You* do." Then she'd reward my effort with a hug and a beautiful smile.

Don't we do the same to the Lord? He gives us clear instructions about life through His Word and wants to lead us step by step in making good decisions. But, no, we get our moral laces all in knots. Even then I can imagine God saying, "Give this to Me. Let Me help." That sounds like pretty good encouragement for us to hand Him our problems with a trusting "*You* do!"

But learning to trust God with the details of our lives can be frightening at times, especially as we're just starting out. I can remember how intense life was for me when I was 19. After my first year of college, I had stopped off in Kentucky to visit my grandparents before continuing my bus journey home to Michigan. Letters from two young men were waiting for me, both demanding a decision. I didn't want to face any more challenges, especially as I was still trying to get used to the absence of Uncle Bob, the Cherokee herbalist who would listen to my laments as he sorted roots and leaves for his medicinal teas. He had died the year before and was buried in Rest Haven, about a mile up the road from my grandparents' house.

One morning, longing to talk to Uncle Bob, I grabbed my Bible and ran to the cemetery, through the stone gates, and up the hillside to his grave. I plopped down next to his headstone and looked toward the river—my beloved Cumberland—as it meandered past its sycamore-covered banks, with early morning mist riding on its brown water, and smoke from the chimneys of wood-burning stoves wafting toward the sky. The scene before me was a peaceful contrast to the turmoil I felt within.

I looked at my Bible and remembered stories of others who, looking for solutions to their problems, just opened the Scriptures and found answers in the first portion they read. But what if I opened to Romans 8:28? I was in no mood to read that God was working everything out. I wanted to know He cared enough to be involved in *this* situation.

So, daring God to encourage me, I decided to open to the *Old* Testament and point to a specific verse. With eyes tightly closed, I thrust my finger onto a page, fully expecting to find a list of begets. Instead I saw Psalm 11:1: "In the LORD put I my trust: How say ye to my soul, Flee as a bird to your mountain?" (KJV).

I gasped. Wasn't that exactly what I had done? Run to this spot on the mountain? I read the words again. God hadn't given me a specific direction; He was just encouraging me to trust the future to Him. That's a lesson I'm still learning.

When my children and I first moved to Colorado Springs, I was astonished by majestic Pikes Peak—all 14,100 feet of it. Every morning, as soon as I awakened, I'd look out the window, marvel at its grandeur, and think, *It's still there.* Then one morning, a rare overcast day occurred, with clouds covering the entire Front Range. But from what I had already witnessed, I was confident that the peak was still there.

God is like that, too. Even when we can't see Him,

He is there. Sure, hanging on to that thought is tough to do sometimes when we're hurting, but what if we practiced thanking Him, not for the situation necessarily, but for His presence in the midst of it? How would our lives be different if we acted out of faith instead of disappointment?

The Power of Prayer

Whenever I think about the teaming of faithful prayers and God's encouragement, I remember a story of Dr. Richard Harvey's pre-med days. It seems that his chemistry professor, Dr. Lee, made a practice of mocking prayer in the class session just before the students were to go home for Thanksgiving break. Dramatically, he would hold a glass laboratory flask at arm's length over the lecture hall's concrete floor and announce that should he drop it, the flask would shatter—and no amount of prayer would keep it intact. Then he would ask if any of the students believed that their prayers would keep it from shattering. Of course, the Christian students would remain silent, remembering the sermons about not testing God. Dr. Lee would smirk, seemingly proving his point. This went on for several years.

Then during Richard Harvey's senior year, with the annual lecture just weeks away, a freshman knocked on his door, introduced himself, and said that he understood that Richard was a praying man. At Richard's nod, the freshman said he was a student in Dr. Lee's class and had heard about the annual lecture. The freshman then gulped and said he believed God wanted him to challenge Dr. Lee when he threatened to drop the flask this time.

"But I need you to be praying for me," the freshman added.

Now it was Richard who gulped, but he couldn't refuse to pray.

For the next few weeks, Richard held to his promise. Finally, the day for the infamous lecture arrived. Richard stood in the back of the hall and listened as Dr. Lee repeated his mocking logic. The professor held out the flask—as he had done for many years—and said that no amount of prayer would keep it from shattering when it hit the floor.

Then he asked, "Is there anyone in here who disagrees with me? Does anyone in here believe that prayer can keep this flask from breaking?"

Richard held his breath as the freshman stood.

"Yes, sir," the young man said. "I believe in prayer."

The professor chuckled. "Perhaps you don't understand what I'm offering to do here," he said sarcastically. "I'm going to drop this glass lab flask onto a concrete floor, where it will shatter. And you're telling me that your prayer will keep it from breaking?"

By now the other students were howling at the absurdity of the young man's challenge.

Smirking, Dr. Lee said, "All right. You pray, and I'll drop the flask." Then to the students, he said bitingly, "Let's get reverent now."

Silence descended over the hall as the young man began to pray, thanking God for His divine power. Then with boldness, the lad thanked God that the glass would not shatter.

At the "Amen," the professor released the flask. Every eye watched it fall. But as it fell, it seemed to turn in midair; then it hit the toe of the professor's shoe, bounced off, and rolled against the lectern—unbroken.

The students sat in stunned silence for a moment, then broke into laughter. The great professor had just been bested. The lecture that had challenged—and often defeated—young faith had itself been defeated.

Dr. Lee never again gave that lecture.[1]

When I first heard that account, I thought, *Well, of course it didn't break. It hit his shoe. It would have broken if it had hit the floor first.*

But that's just the point: It didn't hit the floor first. One brave young man dared to stand up to a mocking professor, and God honored that faith. I wonder what would have happened if a student had challenged Dr. Lee's assumption the *first* year he gave it. Did God nudge someone to stand, but he was afraid? Did God take His hands off the situation until this lad with a pure heart came along? Or did this student "succeed" because he had prayer support? But the greater question is, How would I have reacted if I'd been a student there? Would I have decided "not to cast pearls before swine"? Or would I have stood in faith? I'm losing brain cells just thinking about this in light of those times when my faithful prayers weren't answered in the way I wanted. But those are also the times when we must trust God's sovereignty—and trust Him to encourage us with His presence.

By the way, we've heard that God always answers prayer and that He does it in one of three ways: *Yes, No, and Wait.* But I'm convinced that He answers in a fourth way, too: *You already know the answer!* Think of those times when you have presented a request to our heavenly Father, and suddenly you remembered a solution He had given years before for another situation. And how many times do we pray for something we know we shouldn't have, but we keep hoping God will change His mind *this* time? Those are the times we already know the answer.

Here are some encouraging points about prayer:

1. Prayer is our recognition of our dependence on the Lord.
2. Prayer restores our relationship to God.
3. Prayer releases God's power. (He waits to be invited into a crisis.)
4. Prayer gives us God's peace.
5. Prayer allows God to change the situation—or to change us.

Prayer

Know that life, like Yogi Berra's comment on a ball game, "isn't over 'til it's over." We're going to have heartaches as long as we stay on this earth, so instead of wishing bad things didn't happen, we might as well determine to deal with them in God's strength.

Doing Our Part

Part of my Kentucky years were spent as the youngest member in a four-generation farm household. Our little community was filled with hard workers who prided themselves on well-fed livestock, neat yards, and productive gardens. But one farmer, whom I'll call Abraham, preferred sitting on his porch to working the fields. Every spring, in a burst of energy, he'd plant a big garden, but then neglect it, which resulted in a low yield. More than once, his family had run short of food before the next crop, and he had to beg a few quarts of canned vegetables from the neighbors.

My "waste not, want not" grandmother, Mama Farley, was growing increasingly frustrated by Abraham's routine. Finally, the day came when she finished the morning dishes early, put on her "visiting" apron, and marched down the road to Abraham's house. As usual, he was sitting in a tipped-back chair as he casually whittled shavings from a small piece of cedar.

"Howdy, Miz Farley. Good to see ya. What brings ya over here today?" he asked.

Mama got right to the point: "Abraham, you've planted another fine garden, but it's going to weed—just like other years. You've got a family to take care of."

He barely looked up from his whittling. "Now Miz Farley, the Lord always provides. All I have to do is pray."

Mama's eyes narrowed at that, but she managed to say calmly, "Well, Abraham, I tell you what. Why don't you try praying while you're out there pulling weeds?!"

That situation comes to mind every time I'm struggling with the line between how much is my part and how much is God's. I want to rest in His sovereignty, but I also know that He has placed certain responsibilities in our hands. All we have to do is look at the principle demonstrated in John 11, in the raising of Lazarus. Jesus asked the onlookers at the tomb to roll away the stone (John 11:39) and then, after He had called Lazarus forth, He asked them to "take off the grave clothes and let him go" (v. 44).

Wait a minute. The One who raised a man from the dead was asking the onlookers to roll away stones and loosen grave clothes? Yes, and by doing so, He made the visual point that we are to do what we can do and leave the rest to God.

During my years in Christian publishing, I looked forward to our staff devotions, since the Lord always seemed to provide a special encouragement through the insight of my coworkers. One morning, the speaker retold the account of the longest-running miracle, in Exodus 16. It concerns the manna that fed the Israelites for 40 years. God sent the food, but He didn't put it on the plates; He put it on the ground. Each morning, the people had to take bowls out of their tents, lean over, and pick up the food. Then just before the Sabbath, they had to lean over and pick up enough for two days.

The speaker followed that example with the account in John 9 of Jesus putting mud paste on the eyes of the blind man and then telling him to wash it off in the Pool of Siloam. Again, the one who was receiving the miracle had to do his part to claim it.

A scene I witnessed in a New York church emphasized dramatically the importance of our taking part in our own miracles.

The minister was wrapping up the altar call when he suddenly said, "Somebody here is on drugs, but you can be free. Come down here so we can help you."

He waited; I held my breath. No one came.

Then the minister sternly announced, "Don't you come up to me in the foyer and say, 'I was the one you were talking about.' You get down here and make that confession so we can stand with you in the days ahead. Come on. We're waiting."

Sure enough, a boy of about 15 or 16 started down the aisle. He hated every step he was having to take and kept his tough-guy jaw set—until he was about 10 feet from the altar. The minister stepped forward and opened his arms, and the teen threw himself against him, sobbing as though his heart would break. The miracle began when the Spirit revealed the need to the minister, but the lad had to reach out to claim it. I wonder what encouragement from God we refuse because we won't take that first step?

The Prompting of His Spirit

Years ago, just before we left for the Wednesday night service, I received word that one of my cousins, whom I'll call Eddie, had committed suicide in Michigan. I drove to our church in an emotional fog, mulling over the few details—the drugs, the shotgun blast that didn't kill him right away, the collapse into his mother's arms. And I wondered where his dad had been. Probably drunk. . . . I felt the fury rising as I thought of Eddie's determination never to be like his dad. But then drugs began to dull the hurt in his life, and he was hooked. When he realized that he was mirroring his father, he'd pulled the gun out of the closet, determined that the family pattern would stop with him.

My greatest torment, though, was the destination of his soul. Our grandmother had repeatedly outlined the plan of salvation to him, pleading with him to turn to Jesus. But Eddie was too busy having what he called "a good time." Too busy, that is, until the afternoon when he had seen his dad in himself.

At church, I dropped Jay and Holly off at their classes, then slipped into a back pew. I tried to listen as Dr. Hess taught from the Book of Acts, but scenes of the Eternal Lake of Fire kept darting across my mind.

Then Dr. Hess interrupted himself. "That reminds me of a story," he said, and he launched into an account of the crew of an 1880s whaling ship:

Two of the sailors were Christians who shared their faith every chance they got. Most of the others would either ignore them or listen politely; a few even agreed to attend Bible studies with them. But one sailor cussed them repeatedly, daring them to mention God in his presence.

One afternoon the angry sailor was coiling ropes on the deck just as the ship pitched dangerously, tossing him and the ropes overboard. His fellow crewmen scurried to pull the ropes up, wondering if he would still be in one piece. They'd seen this happen before; often the sailor tangled in the ropes would be cut in half.

As they tugged on the ropes, hauling his body to the surface, they were amazed he was still intact. Even though they thought he had drowned, they rolled him onto a barrel to force the water out of his lungs. Suddenly, he spewed seawater, then coughed, fighting for breath. As his mates leaned over him, he finally spluttered, "I'm saved!" As they thumped more water from him, they agreed, saying they had thought he was dead when they first brought him up.

He shook his head. "No, I'm saved like those two," he said, and he pointed toward the two Christians. Gradually, he stammered the story. "When I hit the water and felt the ropes tighten around me, I knew I was a goner," he said. "And I knew that if those guys were right, I was going to have to face God alone. Just before I blacked out, I said within myself, 'Jesus, I'm sorry. Please stand with me.' Now I'm saved like those guys."

Dr. Hess concluded, "He truly had been saved in those moments and went on to live a godly life. But if he had died in the ropes, the Christians would have thought he had gone to a Christless eternity. We are not to judge the destination of another's soul."

As he turned back to the Book of Acts, he said offhandedly, "I don't know why I told that."

But I knew. Maybe in Eddie's final moments, he had remembered our grandmother's pleas to reach out to Jesus. Maybe the Lord was wiping away tears of regret and repentance from Eddie's eyes at that very moment.

As soon as the service was over, I told Dr. Hess why I believed he had been compelled to tell the story, and I thanked him for being sensitive to the Holy Spirit. He was delighted. Perhaps he had needed some encouragement, too.

Living Thankfully

When thinking of the effect of thankfulness in our lives, I've often pondered Elizabeth Sherrill's presentation at a New York chapel as she told of Chet Bitterman, Jr., a Wycliffe missionary in Bogotá, Colombia, who had been kidnapped in 1981 by rebel forces. While the world awaited word of his whereabouts, Chet Jr.'s father paced his Pennsylvania home, frantic to rescue his son. Suddenly, the thought *Give thanks* dropped into his being.

With his son missing, giving thanks was the last thing Chet Sr. wanted to do. But as he wrestled with this new concept, he realized the command was to give thanks, not *feel* thanks. Wondering what he could possibly be thankful for, he remembered that his son had memorized hundreds of Scripture verses.

Surely those verses are encouraging him right now, he thought.

Then he added thankfulness for his son's physical strength and emotional stability. The list grew. When young Chet's body was found in an abandoned bus 48 days later, the father's thankfulness helped him receive the comfort the Lord wanted to give.

After telling the Bitterman story, Elizabeth gave three suggestions as she encouraged the audience to celebrate daily thanksgivings:

1. Every day, surprise someone with a thank-you.

2. Every day, thank God for something you have never until now thanked Him for.
3. Every day, thank God for something about which you are not now happy.[2]

I had written those suggestions on a 3 x 5 card that I posted above my desk. Now, even years later, I still enjoy the challenge of practicing those touches of thankfulness. And what a difference they can make in each day.

Never Forget Whose Child You Are

We must never forget that because we are God's children, we are valuable. Too often when we make mistakes, we label ourselves failures. Too many times we allow one disappointment to determine the tone for our entire lives. Often as I'm speaking on encouragement's power to offset life's blows, I ask my audiences to say within their hearts, "Because of Jesus, I am a worthwhile person." It always saddens me to see the faces of those who can't say it, and I wonder what causes them to drop their eyes.

A while back, a lady introduced herself to me after a luncheon and said I had spoken at her Detroit church. In that long-ago session, I had given the women the assignment of establishing eye contact with their mirrored images and saying, "Because of Jesus, I am a worthwhile person."

This woman said she hadn't been able to say the phrase even though she had longed to. Finally, she looked into the mirror, took a deep breath, and hurriedly said, "*Sandra says* that because of Jesus, I'm a worthwhile woman."

Then as she talked to me, she smiled. "I'm trying to look at things differently now. I guess it's a start."

It's a great start. And one that will continue to open her to the encouragement God wants to give.

As I think of the many ways in which God has encouraged me through His Word or through special insight, I'm tempted to wonder why He hasn't intervened in all of my crises. But I have a choice here: I can whine about the times He hasn't encouraged me, or I can be thankful for the times that He has. The first choice produces bitterness, the second one ongoing encouragement. That doesn't sound like much of a dilemma, does it? Often it is our heart's attitude of thankfulness and trust that opens us to the encouragement God wants to give, either through His direct touch or through someone else. Our part is not to panic and to remember that He, like Colorado's majestic Pikes Peak, is still there even when obscured by life's clouds.

Quick Encouragement

1. The Lord doesn't promise that we won't have trials, but He does promise to be with us in the midst of them.
2. Sometimes we have to participate in our own miracles.
3. How much better it is to thank God, not for the situation necessarily, but for His presence in the midst of it.

4. Every day, surprise someone with a thank-you.
5. Every day, thank God for something you have never until now thanked Him for.
6. Every day, thank God for something about which you are not now happy.
7. Always remember that you are God's child.

Discussion Questions

1. How do you think you would have responded to Dr. Lee's challenge if you had been in the annual lecture?
2. Describe one of the pivotal points in your faith life. How did you respond?
3. How has that decision made a difference in your life?
4. Have you ever had to participate in your own miracle? Explain.
5. How has giving thanks even in a difficult situation encouraged you?
6. Have you ever felt a prompting from the Holy Spirit to say or do something? What happened?
7. What will you do to help you remember that you're God's child?

Notes

1. Story told by Dr. David Jeremiah on his April 13, 1993, *Turning Point* radio broadcast.
2. Account presented in Sandra P. Aldrich, *From One Single Mother to Another* (Ventura, Calif.: Regal Books, 1991), p. 177.

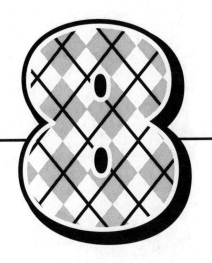

Encouraging Each Other

Jay, Holly, and I were visiting in Michigan when the frantic call came from a neighbor that my sister Thea's house was burning and that the fire trucks were on their way. The three of us and Mother and Dad hurriedly drove the 40 minutes to Thea's, hoping to intercept her before she returned from her son's hockey game. Instead we found Thea, her son, Andrew, and her daughter, Tasha, standing in the yard with their arms around each other. They were watching the firemen direct powerful sprays of water through the front window into what had been the cozy blue-carpeted living room. Thea watched stoically, thankful that her greatest treasures—her daughter and son—were standing safely next to her.

In the week that followed, Jay, Holly, Thea, and I drove back from our parents' to her burned-out home to sort through blackened objects for the insurance inventory. Often I'd hold up a charred object, asking, "What *was* this?" After we listed each item in a notebook, we pitched the item into the industrial dumpster stationed in the front yard. Burned linens and antique books, blackened frames, heat-cracked dishes—all that had once filled her home was thrown onto the ever-growing pile.

To keep from crying, Thea and I tried to find humor in the situation. We had Holly take our picture among the eerie melted shapes of the plastic fixtures and moldings of the bathroom. We made sandwiches in what had been the newly redecorated living room, and when Jay inadvertently dropped a potato chip on the sooty carpet, Thea chuckled and said, "Hey, pick that up. This is the first time I've allowed anyone to eat in this room, and I want to keep it neat."

None of us could undo the tragedy, but we could let Thea know we cared that she was going through it. The Lord is the One who sustains us, but often He works through people to encourage and direct others. That's what all of us should do often in life—take turns encouraging each other.

The following scenarios begin with questions that can be applied to our opportunities to encourage each other. With which ones do you most identify?

That All-Important Thanks

Is there someone you would like to thank for all he or she has done for you? How long are you going to wait before you send that person a note expressing how you feel? I remember hearing about a teacher who had taught at the same high school for 34 years. At his funeral, former students, many of them now lawyers, businessmen, and even teachers themselves, said kind things to the man's widow. One executive in his late thirties was especially expressive.

"Your husband absolutely changed my life," he said. "I'd gotten mixed up with the wrong crowd and was going down a dangerous path. He cared what was happening and took the time to tell me that I had choices to make and that how my life turned out was up to me, not up to the crowd. I'd hate to think where I'd be today if it hadn't been for him."

The widow looked at the man for a long time. Then, with tears in her eyes, she said, "I wish you had told *him* that. You don't know how desperately he needed to hear that he had made a difference in a student's life."

If you know someone who would appreciate a note from you, please don't delay. After all, even a belated "thank you" can offer incredible encouragement. I have several notes like that in my own files from former students who expressed appreciation for my zany classes several years after they graduated. Most of them apologize for not having written sooner, but, hey, I'll take the encouragement any time. And I always write back to let them know what a day—no, *life* brightener their notes have been.

Unexpected Kindness

Have you ever hesitated to offer a kind observation to someone you'll never see again? Does it embarrass you to approach strangers? Years ago, Jay, Holly, and I were on a trip to Mexico with our church. At one site, we were joined by some folks from Mexico City. Our two groups couldn't communicate, but we smiled at each other as our separate guides explained our surroundings.

For Jay, Holly, and me, the trip was supposed to be a reward for our perseverance in adjusting to being a family of three after their dad's death. But instead the trip proved to be overwhelming. The first day, I momentarily lost 12-year-old Jay twice, was cheated in a souvenir purchase, and was constantly reminded by the sight of numerous couples that I was single and alone.

By the time we stopped for dinner, I was convinced I had made a mistake in taking this trip. How was I going to raise two kids alone when I couldn't even keep track of them for a day?

As we lined up for the washroom, one of the men from our group had his hand on Jay's shoulder, making sure he didn't stray. I rested my arms on top of Holly's head, feeling tired and defeated.

Then one of the Mexican grandmothers stopped in front of me, patted my arm, and said haltingly, "You good mama."

Three simple words, certainly, but they carried incredible power. Suddenly, I wasn't so exhausted, and my fears had been replaced with the hope that maybe, just maybe, I could pull this single-parenting thing off after all.

Please don't withhold encouraging comments, even from strangers. You may never know the difference your words make, but I assure you that your thoughtfulness will be remembered.

A Second Chance

That Mexican grandmother helped me when I was tired and discouraged, but what do we do about encouraging someone who has failed completely? We all know that people are more important than things, but what comes out of our mouths when our child drops the serving dish? Or when a relative breaks the ceramic hand off a chess piece we've had since childhood? And even if we do manage to say the right thing, do we hand the item to the erring individual a second time?

I like the story a guide told years ago about Thomas Edison during our tour of his laboratory, which is now relocated in Dearborn, Michigan's Greenville Village. The famous inventor had spent thousands of hours experimenting with incandescent light. Now it looked as though he had at last hit upon the solution he sought. With his staff clustered around him, Edison picked up the crystal bulb containing the filament to be heated by electric current, producing the glow that would push aside darkness. Each staff member held his breath as Edison passed the bulb to his assistant, who would attach it to the stand.

Then the excited, nervous assistant dropped it!

Of course, everyone gasped as they saw the crystal shatter, but Edison merely patted the trembling young man on the shoulder and directed the fashioning of another bulb. When that one was ready, the staff gathered a second time, with the nervous assistant standing on the outside of the circle. But Edison called him forward and handed him the second bulb.

What a statement that made to the young assistant! And what a statement to his coworkers! One of my goals is to get to the place where I can hand the "second bulb" to the one who dropped it the first time. Many times, such graciousness begins with a conscious desire to display that type of gentleness, followed by putting that into practice. After all, we won't react kindly in that all-important, life-changing moment if we haven't been kind in the day-to-day events.

Making New Friends

What do you do when the spouse of your deceased friend remarries? Do you compare the new wife (or husband) to the "perfect" one who is now with the Lord? Or do you take a deep breath and welcome the newcomer into your social group?

A friend, whom I'll call Betsy, was the second wife of Pete, a young man whose first wife had been killed in an auto accident. Betsy and Pete were introduced by mutual friends a year after Pete's first wife died. Eventually, they married and began attending Pete's boyhood church—the same one at which his first wife had been choir soloist for the holiday cantatas.

The first Sunday after Pete and Betsy had returned from their honeymoon, one of Pete's friends slipped and called Betsy by the first wife's name. Then, trying to apologize, he made the situation worse by saying, "I'm sorry. It's just that I'm used to saying 'Pete and Patty.' The names kind of go together, don't you think?"

Betsy nodded and tried to smile, but the implication

hung in the air that while "Pete and Patty" matched, "Pete and Betsy" did not.

At that moment, the friend's wife stepped forward and hugged Betsy. "You need to know that we love you already just because you love Pete," she said. "We're looking forward to getting to know you so we can love you for yourself. We're going to make lots of mistakes along the way, but we hope you'll forgive us."

In that moment, an emotional bridge was built, and Betsy knew she had a new friend who understood the special challenges she faced.

Offering Your Most Precious Gift

Have you ever encouraged a single-again friend? Or does her new status make you a little nervous? One of the many losses for me as a single mom has been the lack of a "sounding board" when I'm faced with a tough decision. When I was first thrust into widowhood, one of the married business instructors with whom I taught suggestively invited me to dinner after I'd asked his advice about balancing my checkbook—a responsibility that had suddenly dropped into my lap. At his invitation, I'd muttered a startled "I don't think that's a good idea" and returned quickly to my empty classroom, where I sobbed at the new, scary world into which I had been thrust.

In the days that followed, I suddenly felt awkward talking to the men I had worked with for years, wondering if all of them thought I was "coming on" to them. Occasionally, a wife misunderstood, too, making sure she stood next to her husband at a social event, hooking her arm through his as we talked, saying in effect, "I just want to remind you that he is mine."

Often I wanted to say, "And I just want to remind you that if he truly is the good man I think he is, you don't have to worry."

My paranoia followed me into a new career where it came face-to-face with the graciousness of Muriel Sandbo, a North Carolina wife. Her husband, Bob, was a board member of the New York organization at which I worked. She called me one day, saying that the Lord had placed me on her heart and even though we hadn't met, she was praying for me because she knew I was in the process of planning a cross-country move. Then she said the most remarkable thing:

"If you need a man's thinking on this, I hope you'll talk to Bob. He's very wise, so feel free to talk to him about the decisions you're facing. I know it must be difficult for a single mom not to have someone to run ideas by, so talk to Bob whenever you need to."

I was astonished—and most grateful. Even though I didn't take advantage of the offer, it was an incredible gift. Her security in her husband's love and her concern for someone who had herself once been a beloved wife came together in an encouraging gesture that opened the door to a deep friendship with her.

Woman to Woman

Do you have a friend with whom you can share the details of daily life? I'm convinced women especially need each other. Our conversations usually include numerous subplots, while men, for the most part, prefer plain, simple facts. That's where having a good friend to share the details of the day is invaluable. During my Michigan days, Nena Batherson and I reserved the first Thursday of every month for time at our favorite restaurant. We'd order exotic sandwiches and flavored tea and finish off the evening with carrot cake. But the important event at each meeting was our conversation. Our problems didn't go away, but talking about them put life into perspective and let us know our struggles weren't unique.

My own experience with deep friendships has been so helpful that I'm convinced if women had more of them, there would be less need for counselors. But too many of us have so many responsibilities that we can't fit one more activity—not even a good conversation—into our schedules. I remember having a double assignment at work that required a lot of overtime; I usually didn't get home until 10:00 each evening. Jay and Holly were both in college by then, so they weren't suffering from my long hours, but I certainly was. I ignored most of my friends and barely kept in touch with my relatives for the 14-month assignment—missing numerous blessings in the process. Keeping up a relationship is much like playing tennis: It's impossible when only one person is hitting the ball back. I wasn't making the weekly phone calls nor writing letters, so I didn't know when my cousins had operations or welcomed a new grandchild. And locally, I didn't supply even so much as a casserole when the sweet elderly mother of our neighbors died. We need to stay

connected to each other. And only by making friendship a priority, the way Nena and I did, can we keep
that connectedness.

The Gift of Good Memories

When you're strolling down memory lane with an old
friend, what scenes do you relate? Once when I was
visiting my parents in Michigan, Bill Coltre, a friend
since fourth grade and now a hometown businessman,
stopped by to say hello. He expressed his happiness at
my writing and speaking career, commenting that he
remembered the wonderful stories I used to hand in for
our English assignments. Soon we were talking about
the careers of many of the "kids" we'd graduated with,
including those who had teased me cruelly about being
from the hills of Kentucky.

"I remember in seventh grade, the word 'hillbilly' was
being tossed around pretty hard in one of our classes,"
Bill said. "You retorted that you'd show us 'hillbilly' as you
grabbed an old dictionary off the classroom shelf, opened
it to the definition, and read, 'hillbilly: a Michigan farmer.'
That shut everybody up for a while as they scrambled to
read the definition for themselves. I was really impressed.
To this day, when my men are doing site clean-up and
find old books, I always look through them to see if I can
find a copy of that dictionary."

I confess I didn't remember that particular scene. (I
do remember the outdated dictionary, though, and have
started my own search for a copy.) What I did remember
from our school years was that Bill had always been kind

to me. And he had proved that kindness again as he chose, from all of his memories of me, one in which I had displayed strength instead of weakness. Certainly his was a remarkable gift of encouragement.

Welcoming New Folks

While we're treasuring long-term friendships, do we ever close ourselves to new ones? I learned the importance of not doing that when Jay, Holly, and I moved to Colorado Springs from New York in 1990. The first day we were there, our new neighbors stopped by to introduce themselves and leave a loaf of homemade bread and their phone number. Then the phone rang, and it was Tom Youngblood, a professional acquaintance who had heard through a mutual friend that my organization was moving to the area and that, in fact, I was the first employee in town. He welcomed me and extended an invitation to speak at his ministry's chapel.

Later, he mentioned my acceptance to Wayne Reinauer, a coworker, who mentioned it to his wife, Nancy, as they prepared for Labor Day guests. To Nancy's credit, her concern wasn't that I was the first of my organization to move into the area, but that my teens and I were going to be spending the holiday alone, unpacking. Her call pulled me out of a dish crate as she invited us to join their party and meet several other families from the neighborhood. That day gave us a sense of anchoring to the town.

My friendship with Tom, Wayne, and Nancy has continued and even survived that awful 14-month stretch in which no one heard from me. In fact, Tom, who travels a great deal with his own ministry responsibilities, has taught me much about balancing a heavy work schedule. He insisted that I see more of the areas where I speak instead of sitting at my hotel room desk, sorting through a briefcase full of files after the conferences. When I took his advice, I began to enjoy incredible afternoons of exploring urban historical districts. Recently, I even bought a Charleston sweet-grass basket from a Creole woman who reminded me of Mama Farley. And to think I would have missed all that if I hadn't been willing to enjoy a new friendship.

From Those We Least Expect

Have you ever refused encouragement because it didn't come from a source you expected or wanted? I've done that more times than I care to admit, and I often wonder how much fresh insight I ended up discarding because I didn't respect the source. A good way to test yourself in this area is to ask yourself how many non-Christian friends you have—not acquaintances, but actual friends, who care about you, worry when things aren't going well, and want only the best for you and your family.

I have such a friend in William "Chilly" Childress. Chilly has encouraged me, scolded me, and cheered me on for almost 20 years, even though he claims to be an atheist (I prefer to call him an "agnostic"). When we were in the midst of my husband's battle with cancer, Chilly, a Korean War veteran, didn't offer scriptures to encourage me; instead, he talked to me as though I were a soldier under fire. I was tough, he said. I'd come through. My duty was to care for Don, and I would do it well.

Of course, I would have loved to have had Chilly's prayers surrounding me during those tough times, but I've learned to accept—and appreciate—the encouragement he is capable of offering. I've prayed for him for years, but he's not ready to give up his view of life and God—yet. Meanwhile, our long-distance friendship continues and often gives me a different perspective on my latest challenge.

My life would be lopsided, indeed, if I limited myself to only Christian friends. Besides, how are we ever going to share Jesus if we don't venture outside of our comfortable and safe friendship circles?

With What We Have

What keeps us from serving the Lord? Often folks say they'd like to serve Him *someday*—someday when they have more time, money, talent, whatever. Encouragement in His name is one way to do exactly that right now. My dear parents, encouragers in their own right, cared for my elderly aunt Adah, who for years lay paralyzed and rigid until the Lord lovingly released her to be with Him. Her hospital bed was in my parents' living room so she could be in the midst of daily life rather than be shut off in some back bedroom.

Numerous relatives and most of her church friends forgot about her, but her minister, Pastor Ron Clark, and two church members, Billie Schneider and Patricia Marsden, often stopped in to say hello. Aunt Adah had stopped talking years ago, and her facial muscles were locked, so visitors had to be willing to give without getting even a grateful smile in return.

Pastor Clark read the Scriptures and then gave Aunt Adah communion, breaking the soft bread morsel into tiny crumbs that she could swallow. Sometimes he also read a simple book with an encouraging theme. Billie hadn't forgotten how much Aunt Adah loved to hear her sing on Sunday mornings, so she continued that ministry, giving a mini-concert for a bedridden audience of one. Patricia offered to visit Aunt Adah when Mother and Dad had a rare social function they wanted to attend together.

These folks came to minister to Aunt Adah, but by providing a glimpse of the Lord, they encouraged the rest of the family, too, by setting examples of practical ways in which folks can reach out to others.

When You Think No One Is Watching

Have you ever learned a lesson from someone who didn't know she was teaching? Have you ever taught someone else in the same way? The most important lessons I've taught Jay and Holly came as they watched me, rather than merely listening to my words—which is just the way I learned from my relatives.

I remember visiting Mama Farley after I had earned my master's degree. As the oldest child in a large family, I had never expected to earn a higher degree, so that coveted piece of paper proved to me—if to no one else—that I had "arrived." I luxuriated in a boot-straps feeling of having achieved the impossible.

The first morning of the visit, I was awakened before 6:00 by sounds from the kitchen. I dressed hurriedly, convinced I had overslept. Mama's hearing had gotten worse over the years, so she didn't notice that I had run down the long hallway and now stood in the kitchen archway to catch my breath.

The room was filled with the early morning sun that poured in through the wide windows facing the apple orchard, and I found myself recalling other such mornings from my childhood. I remembered how Mama Farley had kneaded bread dough or snapped beans for the noon dinner, telling stories all the while. Most of the accounts were of her turn-of-the-century childhood, or of shy smiles over box suppers, or of nervous young men who asked to walk her home from church on Sunday.

But occasionally she'd lament that she had been kept home from school to plow, which resulted in her never having learned to read or write. Then she would smile and say that at least she could sign her own name and not have to make a "mark" the way her father had done. Predictably, she would wave her flour-covered hands at me and insist I get all the education I could.

But that morning, I pushed aside thoughts of Mama's lost opportunities and concentrated on the scene before me. I noticed that Mama's back was a little more stooped and her hair whiter. Everything else was the same—even the round enamel flour pan on the work table and the wood-burning stove. The modern range that her adult children had purchased for her a few Christmases ago sat awkwardly in the corner, used only to heat water or warm leftovers. Mama insisted she couldn't get the same good results from the new oven.

As I watched, Mama pulled a skillet of beautiful biscuits from her trusty old wood-burning stove. I was determined to learn to make biscuits like that. Thinking of the compliments I would receive, I watched her scrutinize the golden crusts. If I turned out such biscuits, I would have placed them on the serving plate with a self-satisfied sigh. But Mama set them in the center of the table and whispered, "Thank You, Lord."

Her gentle words hit me like a sharp rebuke. I backed into the hallway, tears filling my eyes. My life was heaped with material goods, and I had achieved an education that Mama could never dream of. But it had not occurred to me to thank God for them. Right there in the hallway, I whispered my gratitude for my numerous blessings before hurrying into the kitchen to give Mama a hug.

Today her habit of thanking God for even the little things has become a part of my life, too. Now, whether paying bills, planting spring flowers, or pulling a pan of golden biscuits out of my oven, I think of Mama as I whisper my own "Thank You, Lord."

Which of the preceding situations would provide the greatest encouragement for you? Being helped in a crisis? Hearing unexpected kind words? Getting a second chance in a delicate situation? Having a longtime friend remember scenes in which you displayed strength instead of weakness? Being encouraged in a new move? All of these encouragements can strengthen us not only for the day-to-day activities but for those connected to eternity. And isn't sharing our faith the greatest encouragement of all?

Quick Encouragement

1. The Lord often chooses to work through us to encourage and guide others.
2. Even a belated thank-you note can offer incredible encouragement.
3. You may never know the difference your words make to a stranger, but your thoughtfulness will be remembered.
4. Giving someone that all-important second chance may prove to be life-changing for all involved.
5. Women especially need to nurture relationships with each other.
6. Often life gives us opportunities to take turns encouraging each other.
7. Sometimes great encouragement comes from those who don't realize their influence.

Discussion Questions

1. Have you ever received a belated thank-you for something you did years ago? Who sent it? How did you feel?
2. Is there someone to whom you should send a note of appreciation? What did he or she do for you?
3. Have you ever hesitated to offer encouragement? Why or why not?

4. Have you ever encouraged someone who has failed at something? What were the results?
5. Do you have a friend with whom you can share the details of daily life? Describe your friendship.
6. Have you ever refused encouragement because it didn't come from a source you expected or wanted? Describe the situation.
7. Have you ever learned a lesson from someone who didn't know he or she was a "teacher"? Describe the scene.

Grab
Encouragement's
Power

If you've seen encouragement's power in these pages, you know that it's time for you to pass it along. At first, your deliberate attempts at encouraging others may feel a little awkward, maybe even contrived, but I guarantee that the results are well worth the effort.

I've run into some folks, though, who are carrying so much emotional hurt that they think they can't possibly encourage anyone else. Those are the ones who need to hear a story that Dr. Virgil Gulker, founder and executive director of KIDS HOPE, U.S.A., a program of international aid, in Spring Lake, Michigan, told at the 1995 International Congress on the Family in Denver:

> The head nurse of a San Diego hospital had
> a ward filled with war veterans who had lost arms

and legs in combat. She'd tried everything she knew to get them interested in life again, but to no avail. Finally, she realized that their injuries had robbed them of any meaningful sense of contact with another [human] being.

In this same hospital was a ward of terminally ill infants, many of whom had been abandoned. The nurse appealed to the men for help: "These babies are dying. But they have no one to love them. They need you."

Those little ones then began a miracle in the lives of the veterans. A baby was strapped to each man's chest, and the gentle pressure [of the little bodies] was a constant reminder to the men that they were needed. They looked into the tiny eyes of a baby gazing back at them, or watched in wonder as the child slept, or listened to the cries of a baby in distress. Within only a few days, all the soldiers had emerged from depression as they orchestrated the care of the babies—talking to them, singing, ensuring that they were fed and changed. The[se men] were needed by someone else.[1]

In fact, all of us are needed by someone else—even in the midst of our own adverse circumstances. When Jeff's heart condition forced him into early retirement after 31 years as a manufacturing executive, he thought he was doomed to spend the rest of his life looking out the window. But his neighbor, a second-grade teacher whose class was filled with children from fatherless homes, encouraged him to visit her classroom once a week just to read a story and provide a male role model. Reluctantly, he consented, but within the month he felt so needed that he increased his time to three days a week. Not only was he reading a story, but he was also helping several youngsters improve their own reading skills. As in the story of the soldiers, a wonderful exchange of encouragement occurred. Now Jeff has something to look forward to each week, and the children have a positive role model.

Getting Started

Whether your encouragement is dramatic or simple, know that it is very much needed. Here are a few thoughts to get you started on giving your own encouragement.

① Don't Try to Be All Things to All People

Jesus withdrew from the crowds to rest occasionally, and even He didn't try to accomplish everything. Look at John 5 for His example. When Jesus visited the Pool of Bethesda, He walked through the crowds of people waiting for a miracle and walked directly to *one* man to heal him. Now, you let compulsive caregivers like me into that scene, and it would be a spiritual version of the childhood game "Duck, Duck, Goose" as we'd run from person to person, whopping them on the head and saying, "Be healed! Be healed!"

As we face decisions over the demands on our time,

we first need to ask the Lord what *He* wants us to do; then we need to follow His direction. The temptation can be that we think we aren't doing His will unless it's something "grand." I remember thinking about accompanying my Ethiopian friend, Marta, to Africa for a six-week trip several years ago. I didn't want to turn my children over to relatives for even a short time, but I also didn't want to disobey if God was asking me to go.

Margaret Hess, a dear friend, listened to my indecision, which refused to go away even after much prayer, and she said, "Please don't think that just because it's miserable, it must be God's will."

With that new perspective, I stayed in the States to care for my children, knowing that other opportunities would come to serve. And they have!

lower my unattainable Standards

(2) Help People Discard Impossible Standards

At the end of a women's retreat at which I was the speaker, one young woman stayed behind to talk to me. She kept letting others go ahead in the line, so I inwardly began to pray for her—wondering what terrible account she would confess when we were alone. Finally, only she and I were left in the hall.

As I turned to her, she blurted, "I'm not as close to the Lord as I used to be."

I often hear that statement, and it's usually followed by a confession of sin. So, bracing myself, I asked why she felt that way.

She began to twist the tissue in her hands. "I'm not spending enough time in the Word. I used to spend at least an hour studying the Word every morning, but I don't now." Tears were beginning to form in her eyes.

That wasn't what I expected. "Tell me about your life," I said.

"Well, I married four years ago, and now we have three children—three, two, and one."

Astonished, I interrupted her. "Honey, you don't have *time* to spend an hour in the Word."

Retreat speakers aren't supposed to say unholy things like that, so I quickly offered this suggestion: "Perhaps you could post scriptures throughout the house to ponder as you go about your many activities."

She shook her head, so I scrambled for another idea. "What if you were to see care of the children as part of your daily worship of our Lord? As your little ones look to you in trust, that will be a reminder that you are trusting the heavenly Father in the same way." I knew that was stretching the point, but she was desperate.

Tears were threatening to run down the young woman's cheeks. "But I want to be a godly woman like your grandmother," she said. "You've told all those stories about her faith, and there's no way she could have been that godly without spending at least an hour in the Word each day."

I smiled as I opened my arms to her. "Honey, I know Mama Farley didn't spend an hour in the Word each day. She couldn't read!"

At that, the young mother threw herself against my shoulder, sobbing in relief and suddenly encouraged about her daily schedule. The truth about my godly grandmother had freed her from a standard that was quite impossible for her to achieve at this intense stage in her life. I'm also convinced that the truth made her a more relaxed, fun-loving mother.

③ Watch for God's Touch

Each year when it's time to open the new calendar and list all the special birthdays and anniversaries for the coming year, I look forward to a special activity. I turn to each month, plop my finger on a random date, and write the command "Watch for God's Touch" in the space. Then when that day arrives, I'm ready for even the slightest encouragement. Sometimes that special touch comes through an encouraging phone call or letter from someone, perhaps an unexpected rebate check or a double Rocky Mountain rainbow. Sometimes nothing dramatic at all occurs, but I have a fresh awareness of God's presence that allows me to smile and pass along the encouragement to others in my day.

④ Don't Stop Encouraging, Even When Faced with Rejection

Sometimes it's hard to encourage someone else, particularly if we feel he or she has rejected us. In our little Kentucky community years ago, we had the saying "Behind every closed door is a hurting heart." Counselors express the thought this way: "Hurting people hurt people." But it's easy to forget those concepts when we're the ones on the receiving end.

I remember at the start of one school year a certain student in my fifth-hour class who sat at his desk with his arms folded and his blue eyes cold and defiant. Even the newest teacher couldn't have misunderstood his silent challenge. I, as a veteran of more than nine years of teaching, not only caught the implications but wondered what confrontations were ahead.

Sending up a silent prayer, I introduced myself to the class. I explained the material the course would cover and then called roll. Many of the students preferred a shortened version of their formal names, such as "Chris" instead of "Christopher." But when I read the name of the student with the defiant blue eyes, he insisted that I call him by his full name: Kenneth. He quickly informed me that only his *friends* called him Ken. Obviously, teachers did not fit into that category.

Weeks passed without a verbal confrontation, but the tension was noticeable. Kenneth would meet even the simplest request with a penetrating stare and plain stubbornness. He would always wait until everyone else did as I asked before making his move. A slight smirk would then appear on his face to let me know he was complying only because he was ready to do so. Occasionally, he would nudge his textbook onto the floor when I was trying to make an important point. The noise would disrupt the class, and his sarcastic "Oops!" would always draw a chuckle from the rest of the students.

I tried all the normally successful teaching techniques in the hope of having Kenneth take an interest in some part of the course. But I couldn't penetrate the wall around him. Talking privately with him did no good; he merely shrugged, and the same critical eyes would greet me at the next class.

Finally, I concluded that only the Lord could change Kenneth's attitude, and though I continued to pray for him and be thankful he was in my class, I decided to stop worrying about him. Even so, I often found myself replaying each day's encounter with Kenneth and wondering what would help take down that emotional wall.

One Monday evening, while thinking about Kenneth's sullen ways, I poured boiling water over tea bags in a pitcher I'd used hundreds of times before. But this time, the tempered glass shattered, throwing the scalding kettleful of water onto my thighs. Even though I received the proper medical attention right away, the burned flesh formed painful blisters.

The doctor suggested I take the next several days off, but I refused. I didn't want to subject a substitute teacher to Kenneth. I assured the doctor that I would arrange my lesson plans so I could remain at my desk. I told him that my students would be understanding and supportive. But I couldn't help wondering if Kenneth would choose this time to openly rebel, knowing I would be physically unable to assert any authority.

The walk to my classroom the next morning was torturously slow, and I didn't arrive until all of my students were seated. Upon limping in, I was greeted with cries of "What happened?"

I briefly explained the accident to the class. As I did, I thought I saw a flutter of compassion in Kenneth's eyes. I dismissed that thought and began the day's lesson.

The hour passed quickly, and I drew a deep breath, relieved that the class had gone so well. I dismissed the students and began to gather my books and papers for the walk across the courtyard to my next class. Then I realized Kenneth was standing by my desk.

"I thought you might want me to carry your stuff," he said. "I have study hall, and Mr. Kelly won't care if I'm late."

Surely Kenneth was teasing me. But he remained by my desk, quietly waiting.

I gratefully handed him my briefcase.

Kenneth carried my books for the rest of the week, giving me an opportunity to get to know him better. We talked about the weather, his job, and his other classes.

On Friday, we arrived at my next class early, since I was walking better. No one else was in the room. Kenneth placed my briefcase on the desk and stood, head lowered, with his hand still on the strap. Finally, he looked up.

"What degree are your burns?" he asked quietly.

"Only second degree, Kenneth. Why?" I responded.

"I was just wondering," he mumbled. "Mine were third degree."

So my burns are the reason for his change of attitude, I thought. Aloud I said, "How awful! What happened?"

His words tumbled out about the model airplanes he'd loved working on as a seven-year-old, the almost empty tube of glue he'd held over the candle in an attempt to soften that last drop for the delicate wing, the flash of flames, the long weeks in the hospital, and the numerous cosmetic operations.

To emphasize his final point, Kenneth lifted his chin slightly and said, "See? They can't get this spot to heal right, even with skin grafts. I still have this ugly scar. Everybody is always looking at it."

"Kenneth, that is a bad scar," I said. "But I never noticed it until now."

He stared at me intently, wanting to believe me. "Really?"

"Yes, really. Your eyes are what people notice first."

Kenneth gave me a grin that erased all those bad moments he'd caused me during the semester. He turned to go.

"Kenneth," I called, "thank you for sharing this with me."

"That's okay." He paused. "You know, you can call me Ken if you want."

I smiled. "I'd like that very much, Ken!"

That situation occurred years ago, but it still comes to mind when I think of the many emotional walls that can be pulled down by communication and understanding—wonderful forms of encouragement.

Regarding Single Parents

As a single parent, I have a special place in my heart for those who are trying to raise their children alone. For all you single parents out there, please hear this encouragement: First, you *can* do this, if you keep hanging on to the Lord rather than looking for someone to rescue you. The only One who can be all that you need is God.

Second, single moms, get the men of the church involved in your sons' lives. We single women can do an incredible job of mothering, but our sons still need men in their lives. I'm thankful that my son, Jay, has turned out to be such a terrific young man, but he desperately needed a godly man in his life who would talk to him. Unfortunately, there was no such man around who was willing to wrestle with some of Jay's heartfelt questions.

For those of you who are not single mothers, please encourage your husbands to make a difference in a boy's life. We're not asking you to raise our sons—that's our job—but we are asking you to let him come over every few weeks and help your husband change the car's oil or help clean out the garage. In fact, you may even need to suggest such activities to your spouse. Perhaps he's not sure of the difference he can make in a youngster's life. Perhaps he's thought of it but isn't sure how you would react. But please don't pass up an opportunity to be used by the Lord to give direction—and maybe even meaning—to children who don't have fathers in the home.

And I mustn't forget the single fathers, either. When I spoke at a conference in Nebraska a while back, I was amazed that almost one-third of the group was men raising children alone. I'd never encountered that before. I was used to speaking at singles' conferences where my audiences were 90 percent women and 10 percent guys who had come to meet women! But the Nebraska conference opened my eyes to a new need. So, women, *Heather* if there are single fathers in your church, raising daughters alone, you, too, are needed as a mentor.

At the Nebraska conference, one of the fathers stayed behind to talk. He began, "My daughter is 11, and she's, uh, growing up. Uh, how am I going to, uh, buy, uh . . . "

I decided to rescue him: "Feminine products?" I asked.

"Oh, thank you!" was his relieved reply.

Bless his heart! If he can't even say "feminine products," how is he going to talk to his daughter about their use? This is one way the women of the church can encourage in practical ways.

As we near the end of this book, I feel very much like the mother of the bride on their last morning together: "You can't leave yet; I haven't told you everything you need to know." But hear this: <u>We live in a world filled with people who desperately need some encouragement. It doesn't have to be flashy or dramatic. After all, the most powerful results</u> often come from the simplest words.

And, of course, as we'll see in the next chapter, people need us to pass along the greatest encouragement of all—the good news of faith. So, look around you. People are waiting for your encouragement.

Quick Encouragement

1. All of us are needed by someone.
2. Don't try to be all things to all people. Even Jesus withdrew from the crowds occasionally.
3. Encourage others to discard impossible standards and listen to God's direction.
4. Remember that "behind every closed door is a hurting heart."
5. If you're a single parent, keeping hanging on to the Lord rather than looking for someone to rescue you.

6. If you're not a single parent, you can make a difference in the lives of children in single-parent families.

Discussion Questions

1. Have you ever tried to "heal" everyone? What were the results?
2. Have impossible standards ever caused problems for you or a loved one? What happened?
3. Have you seen the truth of "behind every closed door is a hurting heart"? How would encouragement have helped?
4. Have you ever been rejected by someone you wanted to encourage? How did you handle the situation?
5. What opportunities do you hope the Lord will give you to encourage others?

Notes

1. This story is also told in Virgil Gulker, D.A., with Ken Wilson, *Helping You Is Helping Me* (Ann Arbor, Mich.: Vine Books, 1993), p. 36.

10

The
Greatest
Encouragement
of
All

As we are challenged to encourage others, we usually plead that our schedules are too packed. But let's not forget that our calling as Christians is to tell a hurting world about the Lord—no matter how "intense" our schedules may be. Years ago, Burt Reed, president of International Cooperating Ministries, spoke at our church and told this true story that certainly emphasizes where our priorities should be:

> Dr. Paul Stevens, now head of the Radio and Television Commission of the Southern Baptist Convention, was a chaplain at a military base during World War II. He was in his office one day when a man from the air tower burst through the door, saying, "Chaplain, we've got an emergency!"

As they ran across the tarmac, the tower worker explained that a B-17 with a "belly turret"—or gunner position on the underside of the plane—had been damaged in battle to the extent that the crew couldn't get the landing gear down. Nor could they get the turret rotated back into the position that would allow their gunner to crawl out. Still strapped in the turret, he would be crushed when they made their emergency belly landing. The plane had been circling continuously as the crew tried to get the landing gear down manually, but the plane was too damaged.

"They've got two minutes of fuel left," the worker said. "They're coming in now. You gotta talk to the gunner. He's only 19."

What do you say to a young man who has only two minutes left to live?

At the tower, the chaplain grabbed the microphone. The crew had dropped the radio to the gunner so he could talk to the tower.

The chaplain didn't waste time: "Son, do you know the trouble you're in?"

"Yes, sir!" the lad replied.

"Son, are you ready to meet God?"

Only then did the gunner's voice waver. "Yes, sir. When I was a boy, Mama took me to a little church where I heard about Jesus dying for me."

The chaplain could see the crippled plane coming in low toward the runway. He swallowed hard and then said, "Son, close your eyes. We're going to pray. And when you open your eyes, you'll be looking into Jesus' face."

The man had barely started his prayer when the sickening sound of metal on concrete broke through the radio. The plane had made its deadly emergency landing.

All of us are in the drama of that plane—either as the gunner who is moments away from eternity or as the chaplain who knows that our only hope is faith in Jesus Christ. We live in a hurting world that desperately needs to hear the greatest encouragement of all—that Jesus died, was buried, and then rose again, to give us eternal life. And many times, we're the best ones to present that message.

What Do You Say Today?

Jill Briscoe often tells about her work with World Relief that requires her to go into places such as Bosnia or Cambodia and speak to people who have seen their husbands murdered or their children raped and who have lost everything. She comments:

What on earth am I going to say [to them]? I've learned that whatever I say has to be rooted in Scripture; all I'm doing is being a messenger. I'm speaking for the One who has been on the cross and understands.

In Croatia I was asked to speak to a church gathering for newly arrived refugees, probably about 200. Refugees are mostly women because the men are either dead or in camp or fighting. So this group of Muslims, Croats, and a few Serbs had fled to a seminary on the border of a battered Croatian town. . . . We worked all day visiting with the refugees. At night the service was held in this huge, old church, and I had to speak. I didn't know what to say. Everything I had prepared seemed totally inadequate, so I put my notes away and prayed, "God, give me creative ideas they can identify with."

I told them about Jesus, who as a baby became a refugee. He was hunted by the soldiers, and his parents had to flee to Egypt at night, leaving everything behind. I could tell the people began to click with what I was saying. I kept praying like crazy.

I continued telling them about Jesus' life, and when I got to the cross, I said, "He hung there naked, not like pictures tell you." They knew what that meant. Some of them had been stripped naked and tortured.

At the end of the message, I said, "All these things have happened to you. You are homeless. You have had to flee. You have suffered unjustly. But you didn't have a choice. He had a choice. He knew all this would happen to him, but he still came." And then I told them why.

Many of them just knelt down, put their hands up, and wept.

I said, "He's the only one who really understands. How can I possibly understand, but he can. This is what people did to him. He's the suffering God. You can give your pain to him."[1]

In many of life's tragedies, all we can do is point people to Jesus Christ.

Talking with Relatives

Most of us won't have to talk to a man who is two minutes away from death or face refugees who have suffered unspeakable tragedy. However, we do have relatives, friends, and coworkers who need us to tell them about Jesus.

Several years ago, one of my favorite uncles was diagnosed with lung cancer. In the midst of his medical battle, our family's beloved Mama Farley, his mother, died. He was able to attend her funeral in Kentucky but was hospitalized for the last time just a few weeks after his return home. Since he was in an isolation unit, visitors had to scrub with special soap and wear head-to-toe covering to keep from passing germs to his weakened immune system. When I visited him one evening, the nurse warned me that the cancer had invaded his throat, so, though he would be glad to see me, talking would be painful for him.

Covered in the head-to-toe garb, I was concerned that he wouldn't recognize me, so I whispered, "Hi, it's me—San," as I entered his room. His eyes lit up. Kissing his cheek through the mask was awkward, so I patted his shoulder with my gloved hand instead and then pulled the lone chair close to his bed.

"I hate it that you're having to go through this," I said. He nodded.

I paused, wondering how he would receive what I was about to tell him. In the past when any of us—including his own mother—had tried to share our faith, he would wave us away. This time I had to find a way to get him to listen. *Please help me, Lord,* I silently prayed.

"I want to tell you about something Jay said last month when we were at Mama's funeral," I said.

I told him about the long drive to Kentucky during which Don and I had told four-year-old Holly and six-year-old Jay what they would see. We reminded them of heaven and said that Mama Farley—the part we couldn't see—was already with the Lord. Then we told them about the part they would see. She'd be lying in a big box, called a casket, surrounded by flowers, we said. Many people would be in the room, and some would be crying because Mama Farley couldn't talk to them anymore.

Trying to anticipate all our two children would see, Don and I explained that some people would touch her hands or kiss her good-bye in the Southern belief that such action prevented bad dreams about the person. We stressed that no one would make them kiss her, but they could touch her cold hands if they wanted to.

We talked about the sad hymns the people would sing, what the minister would do, and the procession of cars to the cemetery. Then, most important of all, we asked if they had any questions. Jay was concerned with practical matters, such as how the men put the casket into the ground. Holly merely stared at us, her eyes big with silent wonder.

At the funeral home, we gripped the children's hands and walked into the flowered area. I studied Mama Farley's dear, ancient face and thought of the godly example she'd been throughout my childhood. I remembered the skinned knees and wounded pride she had often healed with her hugs and fresh gingerbread. Still years away in my thoughts, I was startled by Holly's question.

"Is she breathing?" she whispered.

We hadn't anticipated that one. And her question required more than a quick no. Suddenly, this business of trying to explain death to *myself* had become difficult. How could I make a child understand?

"Well, Holly . . ." I stalled, searching for something both simple and theologically sound.

Then Jay turned from his study of the casket handles to face his little sister. "No, Holly, she's not breathing. Remember? The breathin' part's in heaven."

A Simple Prayer

As my uncle listened to the account, tears sprang to his eyes.

I, too, blinked rapidly and said, "I know Mama's breathin' part *is* in heaven."

He nodded earnestly.

"And I know I'm going to see her again one of these days," I continued. "I just want to know that I'll see you again, too. I want to know that when I get to heaven, you'll be standing right there with Papa and Mama."

My tears had seeped through my mask. Through the door glass I could see a nurse in the hallway.

"We don't have much time," I said, worried she would soon gesture for me to leave. But the double meaning of the words was evident, too.

"May I pray for you?" I asked. "The words I say are what you can repeat in your heart to accept Jesus as your Savior."

I expected him to shake his head in his old rejecting way, but instead he gave a jerky nod and squeezed his eyes shut. Surprised, I stared at him for a moment; then I put my gloved hand on his arm and began to pray:

"Lord, thank You for this dear uncle. Please be with him; let him feel Your presence as he prays within his heart these words: Lord, thank You for loving us so much that You sent Your Son to die for our sins."

I paused to give him time to pray that within his mind.

"Lord, now I confess my sins and ask Your forgiveness."

I waited for another moment, then said, "And I receive Jesus as Lord of my life. Amen."

We both opened our eyes, and I patted his arm.

Then he mouthed "Thank you."

I bent forward to kiss his forehead through my mask just as the nurse tapped on the window. My time was up.

"I love you," I said as I walked backward toward the door.

That was the last time I saw him alive. He died the next afternoon. Oh, but how much easier it was to let him go, knowing his "breathin' part" truly is in heaven.

That simple prayer was the first time I had led an adult to the Lord. Today, when I speak, I usually offer a more detailed invitation, but its message is still simple.

"Coming to the Lord is as easy as <u>ABCC</u>," I say to my audience. "First, A—Acknowledge that you are a sinner and need God.

"B—Believe that Jesus died for your sins. John 3:16 says, 'For God so loved the world that he gave his one and only son, that whoever believes in him shall not perish but have eternal life.'

"C—Confess your sins. 1 John 1:9 says, 'If we confess our sins, he is faithful and just and will forgive us our sins and purify us from all unrighteousness.'

"C—Commit to living for Him."

Of course, it's important that after the crucial decision is made that the individual gets proper discipleship for spiritual growth, but the ABCCs are a wonderful welcome into the kingdom.

Truly, we live in a pitiful world that desperately needs a smile, a friendly touch, a kind word. Yes, our encouragement can make a difference in the daily challenges we all face, but encouragement also can make a difference for eternity. And that's the *real* power to change a life.

Quick Encouragement

1. We live in a hurting world that desperately needs to hear the greatest encouragement of all—that Jesus died, was buried, and then rose again, to give us eternal life.

2. In many of life's tragedies, all we can do is point people to Jesus Christ.
3. Our encouragement can make a difference for eternity. And that's the real power to change a life.
4. Salvation is as easy as ABCC: *Acknowledge* that you are a sinner and need God. *Believe* that Jesus died for you. *Confess* your sins. *Commit* your life to Him.

Discussion Questions

1. Have you ever been called to share your faith in an emergency? What were the results? What do you hope to take into the next situation?
2. How have you shared your faith with relatives? With friends?
3. Is it easier to talk about your faith to relatives or to friends? Why?
4. Do you know anyone who came to the Lord in the "eleventh" hour? What was the situation?

Notes

1. "Keeping the Adventure in Ministry," interview with Jill Briscoe, *Leadership* (Summer 1996): 111.

Scriptures
to Encourage You

Even with strong faith and good friends, we still can have moments when our human fears and emotions threaten us. During those times, I turn to the Bible for encouragement. I'm drawn to the psalms (especially Psalm 23), to accounts of Jesus' ministry, and to Old Testament stories of courage and victory. Sometimes, though, the Lord uses specific verses to encourage me. The following scriptures have helped me through times of feeling abandoned, confused, lonely, afraid, or tempted. As you ask for the Lord's direction, He'll give you other verses, too.

When You Feel Abandoned

Psalm 119:105: *"Your word is a lamp to my feet and a light for my path."*

179

Isaiah 41:9: *"I took you from the ends of the earth, from its farthest corners I called you. I said, 'You are my servant'; I have chosen you and have not rejected you."*

Isaiah 54:5: *"For your Maker is your husband—the LORD Almighty is his name—the Holy One of Israel is your Redeemer; he is called the God of all the earth."*

Philippians 4:19: *"And my God will meet all your needs according to his glorious riches in Christ Jesus."*

Hebrews 13:5: *"Keep your lives free from the love of money and be content with what you have, because God has said, 'Never will I leave you; never will I forsake you.' "*

1 Peter 5:7: *"Cast all your anxiety on him because he cares for you."*

When You Feel Confused

Psalm 37:5–9: *"Commit your way to the LORD; trust in him and he will do this: He will make your righteousness shine like the dawn, the justice of your cause like the noonday sun. Be still before the LORD and wait patiently for him; do not fret when men succeed in their ways, when they carry out their wicked schemes. Refrain from anger and turn from wrath; do not fret—it leads only to evil. For evil men will be cut off, but those who hope in the LORD will inherit the land."*

Psalm 121:1–2: *"I lift up my eyes to the hills— where does my help come from? My help comes from the LORD, the Maker of heaven and earth."*

Proverbs 3:5–6: *"Trust in the LORD with all your heart and lean not on your own understanding; in all your ways acknowledge him, and he will make your paths straight."*

Proverbs 16:3: *"Commit to the LORD whatever you do, and your plans will succeed."*

Jeremiah 33:3: *" 'Call to me and I will answer you and tell you great and unsearchable things you do not know.' "*

Philippians 4:6–7: *"Do not be anxious about anything, but in everything, by prayer and petition, with thanksgiving, present your requests to God. And the peace of God, which transcends all understanding, will guard your hearts and your minds in Christ Jesus."*

Hebrews 13:8: *"Jesus Christ is the same yesterday and today and forever."*

When You Feel Lonely

Psalm 5:3: *"In the morning, O LORD, you hear my voice; in the morning I lay my requests before you and wait in expectation."*

Psalm 27:14: *"Wait for the LORD; be strong and take heart and wait for the LORD."*

Psalm 37:4: *"Delight yourself in the LORD and he will give you the desires of your heart."*

Psalm 121:3: *"He will not let your foot slip—he who watches over you will not slumber; indeed, he who watches over Israel will neither slumber nor sleep."*

Jeremiah 31:3: *"The LORD appeared to us in the past, saying: 'I have loved you with an everlasting love; I have drawn you with loving-kindness.'"*

Romans 8:38–39: *"For I am convinced that neither death nor life, neither angels nor demons, neither the present nor the future, nor any powers, neither height nor depth, nor anything else in all creation, will be able to separate us from the love of God that is in Christ Jesus our Lord."*

When You Feel Afraid

Psalm 27:1: *"The LORD is my light and my salvation—whom shall I fear? The LORD is the stronghold of my life—of whom shall I be afraid?"*

Psalm 91:9–12: *"If you make the Most High your dwelling—even the LORD, who is my refuge—then no harm will befall you, no disaster will come near your tent. For he will command his angels concerning you to guard you in all your ways; they will lift you up in their hands, so that you will not strike your foot against a stone."*

Psalm 91:14–15: *" 'Because he loves me,' says the LORD, 'I will rescue him; I will protect him, for he acknowledges my name. He will call upon me, and I will answer him; I will be with him in trouble, I will deliver him and honor him.' "*

Psalm 118:6–7: "*The LORD is with me; I will not be afraid. What can man do to me? The LORD is with me; he is my helper. I will look in triumph on my enemies.*"

Isaiah 41:10: "*So do not fear, for I am with you; do not be dismayed, for I am your God. I will strengthen you and help you; I will uphold you with my righteous right hand.*"

Nahum 1:7: "*The LORD is good, a refuge in times of trouble. He cares for those who trust in him.*"

John 14:27: " *'Peace I leave with you; my peace I give you. I do not give to you as the world gives. Do not let your hearts be troubled and do not be afraid.' "*

Philippians 4:12–13: "*I know what it is to be in need, and I know what it is to have plenty. I have learned the secret of being content in any and every situation, whether well fed or hungry, whether living in plenty or in want. I can do everything through him who gives me strength.*"

Hebrews 13:6: "*So we say with confidence, 'The Lord is my helper; I will not be afraid. What can man do to me?' "*

When You Feel Tempted

Psalm 119:11: "*I have hidden your word in my heart that I might not sin against you.*"

Proverbs 28:20: *"A faithful man will be richly blessed, but one eager to get rich will not go unpunished."*

John 14:15: *" 'If you love me, you will obey what I command.' "*

Acts 24:16: *"So I strive always to keep my conscience clear before God and man."*

Romans 12:1–2: *"Therefore, I urge you, brothers, in view of God's mercy, to offer your bodies as living sacrifices, holy and pleasing to God—this is your spiritual act of worship. Do not conform any longer to the pattern of this world, but be transformed by the renewing of your mind. Then you will be able to test and approve what God's will is—his good, pleasing and perfect will."*

1 Corinthians 6:19–20: *"Do you not know that your body is a temple of the Holy Spirit, who is in you, whom you have received from God? You are not your own; you were bought at a price. Therefore honor God with your body."*

1 Corinthians 10:13: *"No temptation has seized you except what is common to man. And God is faithful; he will not let you be tempted beyond what you can bear. But when you are tempted, he will also provide a way out so that you can stand up under it."*

Ephesians 5:8: *"For you were once darkness, but now you are light in the Lord. Live as children of light."*

Philippians 4:8: *"Finally, brothers, whatever is true, whatever is noble, whatever is right, whatever is pure, whatever is lovely, whatever is admirable—if anything is excellent or praiseworthy—think about such things."*

James 1:12: *"Blessed is the man who perseveres under trial, because when he has stood the test, he will receive the crown of life that God has promised to those who love him."*

James 1:22: *"Do not merely listen to the word, and so deceive yourselves. Do what it says."*

1 John 4:4: *"You, dear children, are from God and have overcome them [the spirits of the world], because the one who is in you is greater than the one who is in the world."*

Recommended Reading

Here are a few of the many books that have encouraged me during difficult times. Check with your Christian bookstore for more titles.

Adams, J. E. *From Forgiven to Forgiving.* Wheaton, Ill.: Victor Books, 1989.

Adkins, Mike. *A Man Called Norman.* Colorado Springs, Colo.: Focus on the Family, 1987.

Aldrich, Sandra P. *Living Through the Loss of Someone You Love.* Ventura, Calif.: Gospel Light/Regal Books, 1990.

_____. *From One Single Mother to Another.* Ventura, Calif.: Gospel Light/Regal Books, 1991.

Allender, Dan. *The Wounded Heart.* Colorado Springs, Colo.: NavPress, 1990.

Barnes, Emilie. *Survival for Busy Women*. Eugene, Ore.: Harvest House, 1993.

Bigliardi, Patricia. *Beyond the Hidden Pain of Abortion*. Lynnwood, Wash.: Aglow Publications, 1994.

Brestin, Dee. *The Friendships of Women*. Wheaton, Ill.: Victor Books, 1988.

Briles, Judith. *Money Guide for Christian Women*. Ventura, Calif.: Gospel Light/Regal Books, 1991.

Bruner, Kurt. *Responsible Living*. Chicago: Moody Press, 1992.

Clairmont, Patsy. *God Uses Cracked Pots*. Colorado Springs, Colo.: Focus on the Family, 1991.

_____. *Normal Is Just a Setting on Your Dryer.* Colorado Springs, Colo.: Focus on the Family, 1993.

Cloud, Henry, and John Townsend. *Boundaries*. Grand Rapids: Zondervan, 1992.

Coleman, William. *Before I Give You Away*. Minneapolis: Bethany House, 1995.

Crabb, Lawrence. *Inside Out*. Colorado Springs, Colo.: NavPress, 1988.

Dobson, James C. *The New Dare to Discipline*. Irving, Tex.: Word Books, 1994.

_____. *Emotions: Can You Trust Them?* Ventura, Calif.: Gospel Light/Regal Books, 1984.

_____. *Love Must Be Tough*. Irving, Tex.: Word Books, 1983.

_____. *When God Doesn't Make Sense*. Wheaton, Ill.: Tyndale House, 1993.

Doud, Guy. *Molder of Dreams*. Colorado Springs, Colo.: Focus on the Family, 1990.

Dravecky, Dave, and Jan Dravecky. *When You Can't Come Back*. San Francisco: HarperCollins, 1993.

Duin, Julia. *Purity Makes the Heart Grow Stronger: Sexuality and the Single Christian*. Ann Arbor, Mich.: Vine Books, 1988.

Evans, Tony. *Guiding Your Family in a Misguided World*. Colorado Springs, Colo.: Focus on the Family, 1991.

Fuller, Cheri. *The Mother's Guide of Wit and Wisdom*. Colorado Springs, Colo.: NavPress, 1995.

Gulker, Virgil, with Ken Wilson. *Helping You Is Helping Me*. Ann Arbor, Mich.: Vine Books, 1993.

Houtz, Elsa. *The Working Mother's Guide to Sanity*. Eugene, Ore.: Harvest House, 1989.

James, Kay Coles. *Never Forget*. Grand Rapids: Zondervan, 1992.

Jenkins, Jerry. *Still the One*. Colorado Springs, Colo.: Focus on the Family, 1994.

——————. *As You Leave Home*. Colorado Springs, Colo.: Focus on the Family, 1993.

Johnson, Greg, and Mike Yorkey. *Faithful Parents, Faithful Kids*. Wheaton, Ill.: Tyndale House, 1993.

——————. *The Second Decade of Love*. Wheaton, Ill.: Tyndale House, 1994.

Kent, Carol. *Tame Your Fears*. Colorado Springs, Colo.: NavPress, 1993.

Kraft, Vickie. *The Influential Woman*. Irving, Tex.: Word Books, 1992.

Lucado, Max. *He Still Moves Stones*. Irving, Tex.: Word Books, 1993.

Lush, Jean. *Women and Stress*. Grand Rapids: Revell, 1992.

Maxwell, John. *Developing the Leader Within You*. Nashville: Thomas Nelson, 1993.

Merrill, Dean. *Another Chance: How God Overrides Our Big Mistakes*. Grand Rapids: Zondervan, 1981.

——————. *Wait Quietly*. Wheaton, Ill.: Tyndale House, 1994.

Miller, Kevin, and Karen Miller. *More Than You and Me*. Colorado Springs, Colo.: Focus on the Family, 1994.

Minirth, Frank B., et al. *Passages of Marriage*. Nashville: Thomas Nelson, 1991.

Mowday-Rabey, Lois. *The Snare: Avoiding Emotional and Sexual Entanglements*. Colorado Springs, Colo.: NavPress, 1988.

O'Connor, Lindsey. *Working at Home*. Eugene, Ore.: Harvest House, 1990.

Ogilvie, Lloyd. *The Heart of God*. Ventura, Calif.: Gospel Light/Regal Books, 1994.

Schaeffer, Edith. *A Celebration of Marriage*. Grand Rapids: Baker Books, 1994.

Thomas, Cal. *The Things That Matter Most*. San Francisco: HarperCollins, 1994.

Trent, John. *LifeMapping*. Colorado Springs, Colo.: Focus on the Family, 1994.

Wright, H. Norman. *The Power of a Parent's Words*. Ventura, Calif.: Gospel Light/Regal Books, 1991.

Yorkey, Mike. *Saving Money Any Way You Can*. Ann Arbor, Mich.: Servant Books, 1994.

renewing
the heart ™

Focus on the Family's collection for women

Focus on the Family's "Renewing the Heart" conference has encouraged, uplifted and provided renewal to thousands of women of all ages. And the "Renewing the Heart" selection of books will do the same!

Written by some of the finest women writers, these books feature sound, scriptural advice and teaching on topics that are relevant to today, like personal value and worth, security, ways to nurture and enhance relationships, and more. Best of all, they're from Focus on the Family. So you can be sure you'll be inspired, encouraged, and better equipped to handle the challenges you face . . . and uplift other women you know.

Under His Wings

When tough circumstances come closing in, we tend to make a beeline for comfort, whether it be the couch, the refrigerator, or the nearest shopping mall. But what we don't often realize is that our behavior is based on the need to find shelter. Through tender, poignant stories, favorite speaker and author Patsy Clairmont helps us step out from our secret sanctuaries to face our hurts, do our part, and let God take care of the rest. Only then will we find true healing and refuge. Hardcover and book-on-cassette.

Then God Created Woman

It's a simple fact: women are relational beings. Yet when it's intimacy we crave, we often turn to those who simply cannot fulfill our expectations. Realizing this, author and psychologist Deborah Evans takes readers back to the Garden of Eden to identify all women's deepest need—a close, intimate relationship with the Lord. For only when we wholly rely on God will we find freedom as the beautiful, confident creations He intended us to be: reflections of Himself. Paperback.

Kindred Hearts

All mothers and daughters share a deep, inner longing to be respected, cherished and adored *by one another.* And there's good news! Regardless of whether your present relationships couldn't be better or are less than ideal, you *can* fulfill that need. With keen insights and practical exercises, author Debra Evans helps women of all ages satisfy their yearnings for closeness with the people they're most intimately connected to—their mothers and daughters. Paperback.

To request these or other resources, or for information on Renewing the Heart conferences for women, simply call 1-800-A-FAMILY, or write to Focus on the Family, Colorado Springs, CO 80995. Friends in Canada may call 1-800-661-9800 or write Focus on the Family, P.O. Box 9800, Stn. Terminal, Vancouver, B.C. V6B 4G3. You may also visit our website: www.family.org, to learn more about the ministry or to find out if there is a Focus on the Family office in your country. We are here for you!

Check your local Christian bookstore for these and other Focus on the Family resources.

8BPXMP

Welcome to the Family!

Whether you received this book as a gift, borrowed it from a friend, or purchased it yourself, we're glad you read it! It's just one of the many helpful, insightful and encouraging resources produced by Focus on the Family.

In fact, that's what Focus on the Family is all about—providing inspiration, information and biblically based advice to people in all stages of life.

It began in 1977 with the vision of one man, Dr. James Dobson, a licensed psychologist and author of 16 best-selling books on marriage, parenting, and family. Alarmed by the societal, political, and economic pressures that were threatening the existence of the American family, Dr. Dobson founded Focus on the Family with one employee—an assistant—and a once-a-week radio broadcast, aired on only 36 stations.

Now an international organization, Focus on the Family is dedicated to preserving Judeo-Christian values and strengthening the family through more than 70 different ministries, including eight separate daily radio broadcasts; television public service announcements; 11 publications; and a steady series of books and award-winning films and videos for people of all ages and interests.

Recognizing the needs of, as well as the sacrifices and important contribution made by, such diverse groups as educators, physicians, attorneys, crisis pregnancy center staff and single parents, Focus on the Family offers specific outreaches to uphold and minister to these individuals, too. And it's all done for one purpose, and one purpose only: to encourage and strengthen individuals and families through the life-changing message of Jesus Christ.

For more information about the ministry, or if we can be of help to your family, simply write to Focus on the Family, Colorado Springs, CO 80995 or call 1-800-A-FAMILY (1-800-232-6459). Friends in Canada may write Focus on the Family, P.O. Box 9800, Stn. Terminal, Vancouver, B.C. V6B 4G3 or call 1-800-661-9800. You may also visit our website: www.family.org, to learn more about the ministry or to find out if there is a Focus on the Family office in your country.

We are here for you!